OUR
READERS RAVE

Some books you read print fancy reviews written by fancy book critics. Borrring! At the BRI, we care more about what our faithful readers have to say.

"Hey BRI staff! I think your books are the greatest. I have only one book, but I want more—this is like my fifth time reading it. Thanks for being the best authors!"
— Jessica G., age 11

"You people in the BRI are great! I'm 12 years old from the Philippines and I really like your books! I started reading this summer and it really helped me a lot!"
— Diego de R., age 13

"I just finished your Bathroom Reader for Kids Only and I must congratulate you! There was so much interesting information! Kudos to Uncle John, Elbow Room, and all the hard workers at the Bathroom Readers' Institute!"
— Jonny S, age 11

"I love your books so much that I find myself giving excuses to use the bathroom! Thank you BRI!"
— Kate, age 12

"I love your books! They are really educational. Even my mom reads them! Go with the flow!"
— Ally, age 10

"Your books are so awesome. My aunt bought me *For Kids Only* as a Christmas present, and I'm glad she did. I have not been able to put it down."

—Amber Y., age 15

"I am 12 years old and I LOVE your books SOOOO flushing much!!!!!! They are the best."

—Emily W., age 13

"Wow, you guys are awesome!!!!! I especially love the running feet. They keep me entertained for hours!! Thanks for the great reading material, and keep up the good work!!! I love you guys!!!"

—Shelly O'H., age 12

"I've learned so much from your books. I think you should start a homeschooling course (toilet-schooling?). The Bathroom Reader is more educational than school."

—James B., age 12

"I love this stuff! I'm a third grade teacher, and I'm constantly looking for sources of material to get my kids interested in reading. I use your book to stimulate my kids in the morning."

—Keith G.

"I've used your books to do essays, win contests, and even to do a book report (I got an A+ on it, thanks). My B-day is in March, and what I asked for was…a Bathroom Reader."

—Jacob H., age 9

Uncle John's

TOP SECRET

By the Bathroom Readers' Institute

Bathroom Readers' Press
Ashland, Oregon

UNCLE JOHN'S BATHROOM TOP SECRET
BATHROOM READER® FOR KIDS ONLY

For information, write:
Bathroom Readers' Institute
P.O. Box 1117, Ashland, OR 97520
www.bathroomreader.com

Cover design and illustration by Pete Whitehead
Interior design by Align Visual Arts & Communication
Illustrated by Pete Whitehead

ISBN-13: 978-1-62686-047-6 / ISBN-10: 1-62686-047-5

Library of Congress Cataloging-in-Publication Data
Uncle John's top secret bathroom reader for kids only!. -- Collectible edition.
    pages cm
  ISBN 978-1-62686-047-6 (hard cover)
  1. Wit and humor, Juvenile. 2. Curiosities and wonders--Juvenile literature. I. Bathroom Readers' Institute (Ashland, Or)
PN6166.U63 2014
  081--dc23
                        2013028133

Printed in the United States of America
First Printing: 2014

19 18 17 16 15 14   6 5 4 3 2 1

THANK YOU!

The Bathroom Readers' Institute thanks those people whose help has made this book possible.

Gordon Javna
Kim T. Griswell
Jeff Altemus
Trina Janssen
Jay Newman
Brian Boone
Jahnna Beecham
Malcolm Hillgartner
Thom Little
Laura BlackFeather
Angela Kern
Sydney Stanley
Julia Papps
Paul Stanley
Rick Rebhun
Lisa Priber
Jeorgine Lidelle
Joe Diehl
Lori Larson
Amy Briggs
Sharilyn Hovind

Maggie McLaughlin
Bryan Henry
Scarab Media
John Dollison
JoAnn Padgett
Bernadette Baillie
Kristin Marley
Mana Manzavi
Allen Orso
Gideon and Sam
Kelly Padgett
Max Brunsfeld
Melinda Allman
Brandon Walker
Blake Mitchum
R. R. Donnelley
Dash and Skye
John Javna
Maggie Javna
Porter the Wonder Dog
Thomas Crapper

"Outside of a dog a book is man's best friend.
Inside of a dog it's too dark to read."
—**Groucho Marx**

vi

TABLE OF CONTENTS

Because the BRI understands your reading needs, we've
divided the contents by length as well as subject:
Short—A quick read
Medium—2 pages
Long—3 to 5 pages (that's not too long, is it?)

BOO!
Short
Monster Giggles..................... 237

Medium
Ghost Town............................. 23
Monster Match....................... 217

Long
Ghosts in the
    White House......................... 70
The Ghost of Number 17.......... 169

EW...GROSS!
Short
Fugu! 27
Fart Proudly..............................34
Gassy Poetry.............................69
Ode to a Fart 211
Snot Rags 216
Fart Songs 247

Medium
Guess I'll Go Eat Worms.......... 142
Maggots 193

TRY THIS AT HOME
Short
Changelings............................ 198
Cooking with Uncle John.......... 233

Medium
Games Rule! 147
Home Alone Games................ 261

THE NAME GAME
Short
Familiar Names 21
Name That God 128
Familiar Names 191

Medium
Also Known As..........................43

Computer Speak..........................58
Named After a Kid.....................67

AMAZING KIDS
Medium
A Kid's Choice 51
Richie's Toys 257
Amazing Kids 266
Long
Wild Kids 91
Hot Shots 125
Kid Artists 195

AROUND THE WORLD
Short
Where's the Potty?.................... 28
Where's the Potty?...................204
Medium
The Great Pebble 117
Ice Hotels............................... 252
Long
Seven Ancient Wonders........... 187
We Dig Tut! 272

ANIMAL CRACKERS
Short
Rescue Turtle...........................101
Hot Dawgs 238
Medium
Gullfriends 65

Pocket Pet 175
Long
Animal Antics 38
Fish Fright 102
Groovy
  Groundhogs.........................230

PIRATES!
Short
The Jolly Roger 155
Female Pirates..........................192
Medium
A Pirate's Life 56
Pirate Style 244
Long
Famous Pirates....................... 109
The Money Pit 178

GOOFY GROWNUPS
Short
Dumberer Crooks.................... 149
Crazy Teachers 224
Looney Laws 248
Medium
Dumb Crooks 15
Mr. Eat-It-All 53
Long
Weird Jobs 83
Stunt Masters.......................... 172

V.I.P.S
(VERY INTERESTING PEOPLE)

Short

Classical Kook........................... 87
Uncle Sam 228

Medium

Lion Hunters........................... 144

Long

Who Was Leonardo?.................219

MATHEMAGICAL

Short

Math Magic 17
More Math Magic.....................134

DON'T TELL ANYONE

Medium

Secret Message 63
Secret Places 123
Invisible Ink 163

Long

Treasure Hunt............................ 18
Secret Agent Woman...............254

MEET YOUR BODY

Short

Body Talk 14
Navel Gazing...........................229

Medium

Belly Buttons 95
Body of Water...........................153

WATCH IT!

Short

Aye Caramba! 45
Video Treasures 271

Medium

Scooby-Doo 29
Get Real!...................................99

Long

The Wizard of Oops............... 138

POP SCIENCE

Short

Water World.............................42

Medium

The Write Stuff 35
Ask the Experts 88
Volcano!....................................157

Long

In the Future... 60
Trek*nology.............................. 113
The Bean Car...........................239

RECORD BREAKERS

Short

Record Breakers....................... 112
Throne Awards......................... 141
Record Breakers..................... 183

Medium

The L-o-n-g-e-s-t... 25
More "Longests".....................242

Long

First Ladies 208

WORDPLAY
Short
Flyboy Slang 37
Word Play............................... 119
Page of Sevens........................ 177
Over and Out........................... 186
Palindromes............................ 223

Medium
Why We Say It 81
Acronym Quiz............................97

LIFE IS STRANGE
Short
Bite the Wax Tadpole 55
Weird News 203
I Saw the Potato 236

Medium
Amazing Coincidences 135
Back from the Dead................. 184

Long
Message In a Bottle................. 106

THEY SAID IT
Short
Imagine That!............................ 13
Wise Words............................. 90
Straight Talk 137

Word Wizard 156
Into the Future 283

WILD WORLD OF SPORTS
Short
Hoop Stats............................... 168

Medium
The Balloon Farm..................... 46
Strange Sports 120
Dune Riders............................234

Long
Hoop Dreams 78
Shoe 150
Tree Snorkeling....................... 225
Jamaica Bobsled 263

PAGE TURNERS
Medium
Captain Underpants..................249

Long
Lord of...the Hobbits 159
The Alchemist...........................199

MYTHS & LEGENDS
Short
Lucky #7.................................77

Medium
It's Abominable........................ 131

Long
Mermaid Tales 73

Lost Continent 212
The Magic Horse.....................268
What's Your Sign? 275

TIME MACHINE: THE PAST

Short
Dumb Wars 129

Medium
Meet Me in St. Louis 165
"Hello Girls" 259

Long
Gladiators................................31
Name that Tune! 205

JUST FOR FUN

Short
Knock-Knock.............................22
Riddles....................................41
BEEEEEEP 50
Wacky Holidays.........................62
Cell Phone Tag 86
Ghastly Humor.........................105
Reel Silly 190

QUIZ Answers 284

RESOURCE GUIDE 285

*   *   *

PROGRESS

• In 1900 there were 55 independent countries in the world. Only 9 were based on democracy, and none had universal adult suffrage (meaning all adults can vote).

• By 2002 there were 192 independent countries in the world—146 of them had some form of democracy, and 119 had universal suffrage.

GREETINGS FROM UNCLE JOHN

SECRET MESSAGE #I:
Hotel India Yankee Alpha, Kilo India Delta Sierra!
(To crack this code, turn to page 186.)

SECRET MESSAGE #2:
Yrgpi Nslr lew kew!
(To decode, turn to de page 63.)

Okay, now that all of that top secret stuff is out of the way, we can speak freely (a language spoken primarily by the people of Freedonia, and their leader, I. P. Freely). Hey, let's face it: tons of books are really booooooring. So congratulations! You found one that isn't!

This volume is packed with information about spies and secret codes—always good to know. But there's a lot more: *Uncle John's Top Secret! Bathroom Reader For Kids Only* will teach you how to bark orders like a fighter pilot (*Put on that zoombag, nugget!*) and talk like a pirate (*Aarrrgh, matey!*). You'll find out **who** Uncle Sam was (Hooray for uncles!), **what** it was like to be a Roman gladiator, **where** to search for buried treasure, **when** the pyramids were built, **why** someone made a car out of beans, and **how** ice cream cones were invented. And that's just the beginning.

We're not sure why, but you guys keep asking for more gross stuff, and at the BRI we aim to please. So be prepared—there's a LOT of gross stuff. How gross? We have a farting ghost, a guy who skips the toast and eats the toaster, the sticky history of snot rags, and a recipe for banana-worm bread. Not gross enough for you? One word: maggots. (Don't say we didn't warn you.)

And, as always, we've found a bunch of amazing kids—like the girl who inspired the world's bestselling doll and the boy who was responsible for one of the most beloved books of all time. Plus kid inventors, kid firefighters, and a kid who collected 20,000 hats! And let's not forget the poor girl whose amazingly loud fart caused an embarrassing false start.

So settle in and get ready for one of the best reads of your life. And even though it's *Top Secret*, we won't mind if you share what you've learned. Just remember:

Ks amxl xli Jpsa! Which means...

> *Go with the Flow!*

—Uncle John and the BRI staff

(Thanks Jahnna, Malcolm, Thom, Julia, Jay, Maggie, John G., Brian, John D., Angie, Laura, and my talking dog, Elbow Room. You guys *bark*, er, *rock*!)

This page will self-destruct in 5...4...3...2...1...Kaboom!

IMAGINE THAT!

Here's what some great minds had to say about imagination.

"Imagination is more important than knowledge. Knowledge is limited. Imagination encircles the world."
—**Albert Einstein, scientist**

"Imagination will often carry us to worlds that never were. But without it we go nowhere."
—**Carl Sagan, scientist**

"Imagination is the eye of the soul."
—**Joseph Joubert, French writer**

"Imagination disposes of everything; it creates beauty, justice, and happiness, which are everything in this world."
—**Blaise Pascal, mathematician**

"Everything you can imagine is real."
—**Pablo Picasso, artist**

"What is now proved was once only imagined."
—**William Blake, poet**

"The man who has no imagination has no wings."
—**Muhammad Ali, boxer**

"Imagination is the beginning of creation."
—**G.B. Shaw, playwright**

"There is no life I know to compare with pure imagination. Living there, you'll be free if you truly wish to be."
—**Willy Wonka, chocolatemaker**

Thphthptht! A giant anteater's tongue is 2 feet long.

BODY TALK

Big, small, short, or tall—our bodies are amazing!

DID YOU KNOW?
The human body has enough...

- water to fill a 10-gallon fish tank
- fat to make 7 bars of soap
- iron to make a 3-inch nail
- sulfur to kill all the fleas on an average-size dog
- carbon to make 900 pencils
- potassium to fire a toy cannon
- phosphorous to make 2,200 match heads

DID YOU KNOW?
You...

- blink 9,365 times a day
- fart a pint of gas every day
- use 17 muscles to smile
- use 43 muscles to frown
- shed 600,000 particles of skin every hour (by age 70 you'll have shed 40 pounds of skin)
- can detect 10,000 different colors
- have 10,000 taste buds, which can identify more than 500 flavors

DID YOU KNOW?
In your lifetime, you'll...

- grow 1,000 new skins (your outer skin cells regenerate every 27 days)
- drink 16,000 gallons of water
- make enough spit to fill 2 swimming pools (about 25,000 quarts)
- walk 100,000 miles
- grow 590 miles of hair

Moo-tric system? A cow's moo was once used as a unit of distance in India.

DUMB CROOKS

So you think crime pays? Think again.

LOCKUP

The Crime: A Savannah, Georgia, man wanted to steal guns from the back of a squad car that was parked near a police station.

Gotcha! It was only after he climbed in that he realized his goof: the back doors of police cars lock automatically when someone gets inside. Cops arrested the would-be thief a few minutes later.

TWINKLE TOES

The Crime: Cornered by police in Charles City, Virginia, a drug dealer carrying 12 bags of cocaine ran into a forest to escape. The trees were so thick, he was certain the police would lose him.

Gotcha! The crook must have forgotten he was wearing sneakers equipped with little lights that flashed every time he took a step. All the cops had to do was follow the blinking lights through the forest—straight to the drug dealer.

COVER ME!

The Crime: A person walking by a convenience store in Detroit Lakes, Minnesota, was stopped by a man who needed a favor. The man casually informed the passerby that he planned to rob the store but needed a disguise. Then he gave the person a dollar to go inside and buy him a scarf to cover his face.

Gotcha! The bystander took the dollar, went inside the convenience store...and called the police.

KNOCK-KNOCK. WHO'S THERE?

The Crime: In Hermiston, Oregon, an unarmed man in a red shirt and white hat ran out of a bank with a handful of stolen cash.

Gotcha! Forty minutes later, a police officer searching a parking lot two blocks from the bank heard pounding coming from inside the trunk of a car. It was the robbery suspect. He had planned to make a quick change of clothes inside the trunk, then get out and walk off in his new disguise. When he got locked inside, the thief panicked and yelled for help.

ROADSIDE SHENANIGANS

The Crime: Every police officer has a favorite hiding place for catching speeders. And they almost always work. However, one day an officer got suspicious when every car passing his hiding place was under the speed limit. He drove up the road and found a 10-year-old boy standing there, holding a sign that read RADAR TRAP AHEAD.

Gotcha! A little more investigative work led the officer to the boy's accomplice: another kid about 100 yards beyond the speed trap with a sign, reading TIPS, with a bucketful of change at his feet.

MATH MAGIC

*Astound your friends and relatives with
this simple, yet mystifying feat of
mathematical wizardry.*

PICKPOCKET TRICK

Use this trick to guess someone's age *and* the amount of loose
change in his pocket by having him do this simple math:

1. Take his age and multiply it by 2.

2. Add 5.

3. Multiply this sum by 50.

4. Subtract 365.

5. Tell him to add the
amount of loose change
in his pocket up to 99 cents
(the amount must be less than
$1.00). Example: 37 cents = 37,
which gets added to the sum from **#4.**

6. Add 115.

7. Ask him to tell you the total.

The first two digits will be the person's age, and the last two digits
will be the amount of change in his pocket. Amazing!

Music star Prince is 5'-2" tall.

TREASURE HUNT

Ever dream of digging for buried treasure? Grab your metal detector! The world still has plenty of lost treasure buried in holes and caves...you just have to know where to look for it.

BILLY BOWLEGS' BOUNTY

Treasure: $50 million in pirate loot

Where It's Buried: Florida

The Story: William "Billy Bowlegs" Rogers is said to have hidden hoards of stolen treasure all over Florida during his pirating days. Supposedly there's $50 million worth buried somewhere upriver from Choctawhatchee Bay.

Another $3 million reportedly lies in a secret cavern below Fort San Carlos in Pensacola. According to legend, the old Spanish fort was built with two concealed tunnels leading to a large hidden chamber. One tunnel began from inside the fort; the other was outside the thick stone walls. Billy Bowlegs discovered the tunnels and the secret chamber in the early 1800s, and thought it was the perfect place to hide his booty. Both the Choctawhatchee loot and the Fort San Carlos treasure remain undiscovered to this day.

OKLAHOMA CANYON GOLD

Treasure: $11 million in stolen Spanish gold

Where It's Buried: Oklahoma

The Story: Local legend has it that 200 years ago, robbers hid the gold in a cave in the Oklahoma canyon country, southwest of Oklahoma City. They sealed the cave entrance with a huge iron door

and secured it with a tremendous padlock. Sounds easy to find, right? Yet neither the cave nor the treasure have ever been found. Experts think that's because the iron door and lock have rusted and now match the color of the brick-red clay so common to Oklahoma, perfectly camouflaging the entrance from fortune hunters.

POST OFFICE TREASURE

Treasure: A fortune in gold and cash

Where It's Buried: Southern Oregon

The Story: In the 1800s, the Swan Lake post office served as a stagecoach stop between Lakeview and Klamath Falls, Oregon. It also became a handy place for one bandit to hide his stolen loot.

Here's how it happened: After robbing several stagecoaches, the bandit and his partner decided to split up to foil their pursuers. One went south to California; the other one (the one with the gold) headed east toward Klamath County. Along the way he got worried about being caught with all that loot, so he buried it behind the post office. He soon began to regret his lawless deeds and decided to go straight. He took up farming— and never saw his partner or the loot again.

Years later, just before he died, the old bandit told the rancher he worked for all about his former life of crime. And he revealed exactly where he had buried the gold.

- Stand at the back door of the post office.
- Walk 190 paces due east.

Crocodiles sleep with their eyes open.

• Back up 9 paces (the robber hit a rock when he started digging, so he had to backtrack).

• Step 3 paces to the north.

The only problem: The post office isn't there anymore. Treasure hunters have searched long and hard for the Swan Lake cache, but the loot remains hidden.

PIRATE BOOTY

Treasure: Stolen jewels

Where It's Buried: Southeastern Florida

The Story: Pirate José Gaspar is said to have buried a large chest of jewels in the middle of a muddy lake near Placida, Florida. He used a huge heavy chain to anchor the chest to a nearby palm tree, and he even left directions:

• Begin at the southern tip of Placida Island.
• Go due north through Cape Haze.
• Turn right.
• Go east one mile until you come to the lake.
• Wade out to the middle and start digging.

But beware! The lake is infested with poisonous snakes.

❋   ❋   ❋

TREASURE FACTS

According to experts, 10 years after a treasure has been buried there is only a 50% chance that it will ever be found. The more time that passes, the worse anyone's chance of finding it…so start digging!

Shoes on the right foot usually wear out faster than shoes on the left.

FAMILIAR NAMES

Some people achieve immortality because of their names.
You know the names—now here are the people.

JULES LEOTARD (1839-1870). This famous French acrobat felt that he could perform his flying trapeze act better if his loose pants weren't always getting in the way. So he invented snug-fitting tights, which he named after himself—*leotards*.

JEAN NICOT (1530-1600). While serving as the French ambassador to Portugal in the 1550s, Nicot brought tobacco back to his native France. When nicotine was found in tobacco leaves in 1828, it was named after him.

CÉSAR RITZ (1850-1918). Ritz was a Swiss businessman who owned a chain of fancy hotels. When Nabisco introduced a new cracker in 1934, they named it after the fanciest thing they could think of: the *Ritz*.

R. J. LECHMERE GUPPY (1836-1916). He was a minister in Trinidad who sent several species of fish to British scientists, including one tiny specimen they named in his honor, the *guppy*.

ADOLPHE SAX (1814-1894). Sax was a Belgian instrument maker who wanted to create a new horn that would have "the flexibility of the strings, the variety of the woodwinds, and the power of the brasses." His invention was an instant success that changed music forever. He called it the *saxophone*.

KNOCK-KNOCK

Who's there? These jokes. They may get a bad rap...but we love 'em.

Knock-knock #1
Knock-knock.
Who's there?
Ida.
Ida who?
Ida called first
but the phone's
not working.

Knock-knock #2
Knock-knock.
Who's there?
Deluxe.
Deluxe who?
Deluxe-smith. I'm
here to fix de lock.

Knock-knock #3
Knock-knock.
Who's there?
Cows go.
Cows go who?
No. Cows go
"moo."

Knock-knock #4
Knock-knock.
Who's there?
Panther.
Panther who?
Panther no
panth, I'm going
thwimming.

Knock-knock #5
Knock-knock.
Who's there?
Danielle.
Danielle who?
Danielle. I heard
you the first time!

Knock-knock #6
Knock-knock.
Who's there?
Ya.
Ya who?
Yahoo! Ride 'em,
cowboy!

Knock-knock #7
Knock-knock.
Who's there?
Omelette.
Omelette who?
Omelette smarter
than I look.

Knock-knock #8
Knock-knock.
Who's there?
Comma.
Comma who?
Comma little
closer and I'll
tell you.

Knock-knock #9
Knock-knock.
Who's there?
Saul.
Saul who?
Saul there is—
th'ain't no more.

The art of ringing bells is called *campanology*.

GHOST TOWN

*Imagine a thriving city being completely swallowed by the sea.
That's just what happened to England's Lost City of Dunwich.*

NOW YOU SEE IT...

A thousand years ago the English seaport of Dunwich was the
capital of powerful kings. At its peak during the 12th century,
the city covered more than a square mile and was home to
4,000 people. It had 10 churches, a king's palace, a mayor's
mansion, hospitals, a monastery, and a harbor full of merchant
ships. Perched on the coast of England, it looked east toward
Denmark across the stormy North Sea. But the town's days were
numbered…because Dunwich had been built on sand.

…NOW YOU DON'T

In 1342, the people of Dunwich got their first lesson about building
a city on sand: In a single storm, 400 houses were washed into
the ocean. And that was just a start. Between 1535 and 1600, four
churches disappeared. By 1677 the sea completely covered the
center of town. St. Peter's Church was lost in 1702, followed by its
graveyard in 1729.

 After a particularly bad storm later in the 18th century, St.
Peter's Church and graveyard reappeared. It was a ghastly sight:
The wooden coffins had rotted and disappeared into the ocean
along with the soil. All that was left of the graveyard was a group
of headstones and skeletons scattered across the ground. Then,
just as quickly as the graveyard had appeared, it vanished, covered
again by the sea.

GHOSTLY BELLS

Over the next 200 years, the sea ate away at the rest of the town until the last church toppled into the surf in 1912. Dunwich was gone.

Today all that remains of the ghost town are a few fishermen's cottages that cling to the cliffs. A person standing on those cliffs at low tide can sometimes catch a glimpse of a church steeple peeking out of the water. Even more remarkably, occasionally the church bells can be heard ringing—*underwater.* Sailors take those bells as a warning that a storm is coming and don't put out to sea. It's an eerie reminder of the once-thriving city of Dunwich, now resting beneath the waves.

The first recorded sighting of the Loch Ness Monster? 565 A.D.

THE
L-O-N-G-E-S-T...

Why is it some people will go to any length to be...well...long?

...HAIR

When Hoo Sateow's hair was measured for the *Guinness Book of World Records* in 1997, it was declared the longest hair in the world—16 feet, 11 inches! (His brother Yee came in second at an even 16 feet). Hoo, from Chiang Mai, Thailand, believed his hair gave him magical healing powers. When he died at the age of 89, he had not had a haircut for more than 70 years.

...BEARD

Hans Langseth, a Norwegian who emigrated to the United States, quit shaving when he was 30 years old. Over the next 51 years, his beard grew to an astonishing 17 feet, 6 inches in length. His beard was cut off when he died in 1927 and later donated to the Smithsonian Institution in Washington, D.C.

...TOENAILS

Louise Hollis of Compton, California, decided to grow out her toenails one summer—and she never cut them again. As of 1991, when they were measured for Guinness World Records, the combined length of her toenails was 87 inches—that's about 8 inches each!

Hollis loves her long nails. She spends two days a week painting and filing them but refuses to trim them.

...FINGERNAILS

As a young boy, Shridhar Chillal of Poona, India, aspired to do something "unique and outstanding." So he stopped trimming the fingernails on his left hand and just let them grow...and grow... and grow...for 48 years. When they were measured in 1998, their combined length was more than 20 feet (about 4 feet per nail).

Growing super-long fingernails may sound easy, but it requires great sacrifice. Chillal had to give up any activity where his fingernails might be accidently damaged, including reading, writing, cycling...even walking.

...MOUSTACHE

Sixty-two-year-old Mohammed Rashid of Turkey travels the globe, meeting people and showing them his record-breaking 5-foot 3-inch long moustache. You can have your picture taken with him and his amazing moustache for a mere $5.

...EAR HAIR

Fifty-year-old Radhakant Bajpai of India has bushy black hair sprouting out of his ears—and it's 5 ¼ inches long. He told reporters, "Making it to the Guinness records is indeed a special occasion for me and my family. God has been very kind to me."

FUGU!

Even though some people consider it a delicacy, you can actually die from eating this fish.

SPIKY AND POISONOUS...

Fugu is the Japanese name for the poisonous puffer fish, or blowfish. Instead of scales, the fugu has spines like a porcupine. When it's scared, it puffs up and looks like a spiky balloon with fins.

But the spikes are only half the story: The fugu's liver and intestines contain *tetrodotoxin*, a powerful poison that is 1,200 times deadlier than cyanide. In fact, the poison in one fugu can kill 30 people. Yet this fish is a favorite in many Japanese restaurants.

...BUT VERY TASTY

If this fish is so poisonous, why are restaurants allowed to serve it? They have highly trained "fugu-certified" chefs who know how to remove the poisonous parts. Still, even experts can make mistakes—about 100 people in Japan die from eating fugu every year.

The most poisonous fish, *tora-fugu*, is also the most delicious...and the most expensive. One plate of this fugu can cost anywhere from $100 to $200.

Despite the danger and the expense, the Japanese eat more than 10,000 tons of fugu annually. Dying to try it? Not us—we'll skip the fugu and go right to dessert.

The fugu is the only fish that can close its eyes.

WHERE'S THE POTTY?

There are many important questions in life. Here are 16 ways to ask the most important one.

Hawaiian: *Ai hea lua?*

Gaelic: *Ca bhfuil an leithreas?*

Armenian: *Our eh paghnikeh?*

Portuguese: *Onde fica o banheiro?*

French: *Où sont les toilette?*

Swahili: *Choo kiko wapi?*

Greek: *Pu' i'ne i tuale'ta?*

Zulu: *Likuphi itholethe?*

Thai: *Hong nam you tee nai?*

Romanian: *Unde este toaleta?*

Hungarian: *Hol a mosdó?*

Icelandic: *Hvar er snyrtingin?*

Slovak: *Kde je WC?*

Mandarin: *Xiv shouv jian-zai-na li?*

Italian: *Dove é il bagno?*

Korean: *Hwa-jang-sil-i O-die Isum-ni-ka?*

Louisiana loses 60 acres a day to coastal erosion.

SCOOBY-DOO!

Who's our favorite canine (besides Uncle John's talking dog, Elbow Room)? Scooby-Doo! Here's his story.

SATURDAY MORNING SCARES

In 1969 Fred Silverman, a programming director at CBS, had an idea for a Saturday morning cartoon called *House of Mystery*. It would be centered around a group of teenagers who chase ghosts and solve mysteries. Silverman brought the idea to TV's most popular animators at the time, Bill Hanna and Joe Barbera (creators of *The Flintstones* and *The Jetsons*).

The Hanna-Barbera team loved it and quickly created the characters. They called the show *Mysteries Five*, then renamed it *Who's S-s-s-s-cared?* It was about four teenagers and their dog (who at that time only had a small part). Silverman took the idea to New York and presented it to top CBS executives. To his surprise, they rejected it. Why? Because they thought it would be too scary, especially for little kids. That posed a big problem for Silverman: he had already reserved his best Saturday morning slot for the show. He was determined to change their minds.

A SONG SAVES THE DAY

Silverman spent most of his flight back to Los Angeles trying to figure out some way to sell the show. Finally, to relax, he put on his headphones. The first thing he heard: a Frank Sinatra song called "Strangers in the Night," which ends with the nonsense lyrics "scooby-dooby-doo." Silverman suddenly had an inspiration—*that* could be the dog's name! And if he made the dog the star of the

Celebrity fact: Scooby-Doo is his nickname. His real name is "Scoobert."

show, it would be *funny*, not scary! The CBS executives bought it, and Scooby-Doo was born.

IT'S A HIT!

The show, finally named *Scooby-Doo, Where Are You!*, was an instant success. It took over Saturday morning in the 1970s and eventually set a still-unbroken record as the longest-running children's animated show. Over the next 18 years there were 11 different television series with the name "Scooby-Doo" in the title. Ten other dogs appeared in the series, all related to Scooby. The most famous, but least liked, was Scooby's nephew, Scrappy-Doo. In a recent Internet poll, Scrappy was voted "Most annoying cartoon character of all time."

SCOOBY SNACKS

• A live-action version of *Scooby-Doo* hit movie theaters in 2002. The TV theme song was remade as a reggae/hip-hop song for the movie. It's sung by—who else—Shaggy.

• Considered for starring roles in the movie: Christina Ricci (Velma), Brendan Fraser (Fred), and Heather Graham (Daphne).

• In the original cartoon, Scooby-Doo was almost a sheepdog named Too Much.

• Fred was named for the TV executive responsible for creating Scooby-Doo, Fred Silverman.

Grasshoppers hear with the fronts of their knees.

GLADIATORS

*Today kids have posters of movie stars and athletes
on their walls. In ancient Rome, the poster
boys were a little more dangerous.*

LET THE GAMES BEGIN

The granddaddy of all sports arenas was the Roman Colosseum,
opened by Emperor Titus in 80 A.D. But no games of baseball,
football, or soccer were played in this arena. Instead, 50,000
people would come to watch fierce games of killing and bloodshed.

The "stars" of the games were *gladiators*—warriors who fought
each other in hand-to-hand combat…to the death. Occasionally
they had to fight exotic animals like lions, tigers, and hippos.
Other times, the Colosseum would be filled with water so that they
could fight "sea battles" in ships.

LEARNING TO FIGHT

Gladiators were trained in special schools. Some were volunteers,
but most were prisoners of war, slaves, or criminals. If they were
skillful—or lucky—they won their fights and their lives were
spared. But not always. A wounded gladiator had to plead for
mercy…and the emperor made the ultimate decision.

The first gladiators were captured soldiers who were forced
to fight with their own weapons. Since the men came from many
countries, their styles of weapon, tactics, and dress were very
different. Over time these various looks became associated with
different types of gladiator. Pitting different styles of fighter against
each other made the fight even more exciting to the Romans.

- **Samnites.** Named after soldiers from the southern part of Italy, they wore the most armor. They had helmets with visors and carried oblong shields and short swords. They wore heavy metal guards on their left legs along with protective ankle and wrist guards.

- **Thracians.** Named after the soldiers of northern Greece, they wore little armor and fought with curved swords and small round shields. They were among the most popular gladiators. One inscription on a wall in Pompeii describes the Thracian gladiator Celadus as "the sigh and glory of girls."

- **Mirmillo.** The name means "fish man." He wore a helmet with a high crest in the shape of a fish. He carried a long shield that covered his legs and wore arm guards and metal leg shields.

- **Retiarius.** The "net man" fought with a lead-weighted net and a *trident* (a three-pronged spear). He wore no helmet and little armor. A wide leather belt protected his stomach, and an arm guard with a shoulder shield protected one side of his body. The retiarius generally fought the *mirmillo.*

- **Secutor.** The "pursuer" also fought the *retiarius*, chasing him around the arena. He wore a curved helmet, making it harder to be caught under the net. The helmet covered his face but had oddly spaced eyeholes, making it difficult to see. The *secutor*'s entire left side was protected by a heavy curved shield and a metal leg guard. He wore metal or leather bands on his right arm.

GLADIATOR FACTS

- Emperors and ordinary Roman citizens often "fought" as gladiators in the arena, although their opponents were usually unarmed. Emperor Commodus was said to have killed 1,000 victims this way.

• Women sometimes became gladiators, too. Most were slaves who fought other women or male dwarfs.

• Some gladiators were so popular that they were given gold and other gifts. Emperor Nero even gave a palace to the gladiator Spiculus.

• The ancient Romans believed that drinking a gladiator's blood would make them strong. People lined up with cups to catch the blood of wounded gladiators.

• Most gladiators eventually died in the arena, but if the crowd truly loved a certain competitor, they could vote to free him. Then he could retire in peace.

FART PROUDLY

Uncle John loves fart stories (as long as they're not about him).

BLAST FROM THE PAST

It's bad enough being haunted by a ghost—but a ghost who farts? Workers at a computer factory in England have reported being haunted by a ghost who does just that.

The factory was built on the site of a 19th-century chapel, and workers are convinced the ghost is the embarrassed spirit of a girl who passed gas while singing in church. "On several occasions," says one employee, "there has been a faint girlish voice singing hymns, followed by a loud raspberry sound, and then a deathly hush."

ON YOUR MARK...GET SET...FART!

A girl wrote to a teen magazine with this moving story. It seems she was about to race in a big swim meet. Her boyfriend was in the bleachers, ready to cheer her on. When the starting judge told the swimmers to take their marks, she bent into her starting crouch... and ripped a fart. It was so loud that the swimmer next to her thought the noise was the starter's pistol and dove into the pool. When the judges realized what had happened, they called it a false start and the swimmers had to start over. The girl was so humiliated she could hardly swim and finished last. (The staff of the BRI give this Embarrassing Moment our highest rating—5 plungers!)

T E WRITE STU F

*It's the original word processor. It's very user-friendly: you
can easily delete mistakes, it doesn't need electricity,
and it fits in your pocket. What is it? A pencil.*

GET THE LEAD OUT

Is there really lead in a pencil? Nope. That dark stuff is actually a
mineral called graphite. People call it "lead" because the men who
first discovered a huge graphite deposit in England in 1564 thought
it was lead. When scientists later discovered that it wasn't—it's
a form of carbon—they renamed it *graphite*, from a Greek word
meaning "to write." But for some reason, the term "lead" has stuck.

Using graphite for writing wasn't new—the Aztecs had been
doing it long before Columbus arrived in the New World. But it
was new to Europeans. They discovered that the soft graphite made
rich, dark lines, so they carved pointy "marking stones" out of it.

The only problem with the marking stones: the black stuff got
all over the writer's hands. Eventually, people figured out that they
could wrap string around the stones to keep their hands clean, and
unwind the string as the graphite wore down. And that was the first
version of the modern pencil.

DRAW YOUR OWN CONCLUSION

Today, more than 14 billion pencils are produced every year.
Placed end to end, that's enough to circle the Earth 62 times.
Pencils are now available in varying levels of hardness and darkness.
The number printed on the pencil's side tells you how dark your
writing will be. The higher the number, the darker the writing.

In China, bats are symbols of happiness.

HOW PENCILS ARE MADE

1. First, the graphite is ground up and mixed with fine clay. The more clay added, the harder the pencil lead.

2. Then the mixture is forced through an extruder to make a long, thin rod.

3. The rod is baked in an oven at a temperature of 2,200°F to harden it.

4. Then it is treated with wax for smoother writing.

5. Wood is sawed into very small boards that are the length of one pencil, the width of seven pencils, and the thickness of half a pencil.

6. Seven tiny grooves are cut lengthwise in the boards.

7. Then seven rods of lead are laid into each of them, and an identical board is glued on top.

8. A machine cuts the boards into seven individual pencils.

9. The finished pencils are then painted with several layers of nontoxic paint (so you can chew on them!).

The 50-ton Hoba Meteorite is the heaviest known meteor to fall on Earth.

FLYBOY SLANG

Look here, nugget, check six and don't get beaded up if you can't tell a bogey from a bandit! Military pilots have their own special lingo—here are some examples.

- **Bandit:** Enemy aircraft

- **Fangs out:** Ready for a dogfight

- **Speed of heat:** Fast... very fast

- **Beaded up:** Worried or excited

- **Kick the tires, light the fires:** Let's get this jet in the air right now!

- **Painted:** Scanned by radar

- **Check six:** "Watch your back! Be careful!" (Pilots use a clock system: 12 o'clock is straight ahead. 6 o'clock is directly behind.)

- **Whiskey Charlie:** "Who cares?"

- **Zoombag:** Flight suit

- **Fur ball:** Confused air battle with lots of planes

- **Spooled up:** Excited

- **Bogey:** Unidentified, possibly hostile aircraft

- **Nugget:** Pilot on his or her first tour of duty

- **Pucker factor:** How scary something is

- **Go Juice:** Coffee

- **Wingman:** Second pilot in a two-plane formation (always makes sure the leader's "6 o'clock" stays clear)

- **Goo:** Cloudy weather that makes it hard to see

- **Nylon letdown:** Parachute ride

- **Bravo Zulu:** "Good job!"

Does it bug you? There are at least 1 million species of insects in the world.

A IMAL ANTI S

Uncle John's talking dog, Elbow Room, does a few
funny tricks—but even he can't top these!

NINE LIVES AT SEA

During World War II, a cat named Oscar was ship's cat on the
German battleship *Bismarck*. In 1941 the *Bismarck* was torpedoed
and sank, but Oscar was rescued by a sailor from the British
ship HMS *Cossack*. Five months later the *Cossack* was sunk in a
collision, but Oscar was saved by sailors on the HMS *Ark Royal*.
Three weeks after that a German submarine blew up the *Ark
Royal*...and Oscar was rescued again! That's when the British naval
authorities decided to "ground" Oscar, since he seemed to bring
bad luck to any ship he was on. According to naval records, Oscar
the cat died peacefully in 1955...on dry land.

FOWL PLAY

When small fires kept breaking out near the holy Japanese shrine of
Fushimi Inari Taisha, local police suspected an arsonist was setting
them deliberately. They set up security cameras to catch the culprit
in the act. But the firebug caught by the cameras wasn't a person at
all. It was a flock of birds!

It turned out that crows were stealing candles from around the
shrine. Some of the candles were lit, and when they became too
hot to carry, the crows dropped them on piles of leaves, which
started the fires.

As Hiroyoshi Higuchi, a Tokyo professor of ornithology,
explained: "Crows love oily food, which is probably why they stole

In the Middle Ages, boys began training to become knights at age 7.

the wax candles." The candles were made of paraffin wax, which is made from oil. *Yum.*

HOLE IN ONE

A golfer in Wales hit such a powerful drive on the 18th hole that it shot straight up the butt of a sheep grazing beside the golf course. Imagine the sheep's surprise as it bolted across the golf course, taking the ball with it. Imagine the golfer's surprise when the sheep galloped onto the green... and dropped the ball right next to the 18th hole!

LLAMA DRAMA

Milo the llama takes his job seriously. As leader of a herd of llamas on the Bailey farm in Northamptonshire, England, he guards the sheep and other animals, protecting them from foxes and stray dogs. Milo also looks after his owner, Graham Bailey.

One day while feeding the llamas, the 72-year-old farmer fell and broke his hip. Milo sprang into action. He danced excitedly around Farmer Bailey, leading the other llamas in a circle formation. There they stayed, like an honor guard while Bailey yelled for help. Two hours later, a dog walker heard Bailey and called for an ambulance.

About 4,000 stars are visible from Earth without a telescope.

Unfortunately, the llamas didn't know the ambulance crew was there to help their owner. They kicked fiercely at the paramedics to keep them away from Bailey. The medics had to call for an air ambulance as backup. That did it. Milo and the llamas stampeded away from the strange hovering craft...and Farmer Bailey was rescued.

JAILBIRDS

As far back as the Roman Empire, geese have been used as guards. Historians point to the events of 390 B.C., when a group of temple geese sounded the alarm as barbarian troops surprise-attacked Rome. This gave the Romans enough time to mount a defense. It may sound far-fetched, but it makes sense—geese have exceptional eyesight, and they honk loudly at strangers.

So in 1992, when authorities at the Berga prison in Sweden brought in 20 guard geese, everyone thought it was a pretty good plan. Now the prison would have low-cost guards who would never get bored patrolling the fences of the prison. And they could be counted on to raise a noisy racket if a prisoner tried to escape.

Everything went well until the warden put prisoners in charge of feeding the geese. The birds quickly shifted their loyalty to their feeders and would honk angrily whenever the guards came near. And when a group of prisoners tried to escape, the geese let them by without making a single honk. Result: The geese were retired from guard duty. Now their only job is to provide eggs for breakfast.

RIDDLES

*See if you can stump your friends
with these classic riddles.*

Q: What room has no door, no windows, no floor, and no roof?
A: A mushroom.

Q: What starts with "e" and ends with "e" and contains only one letter?
A: An envelope.

Q: What did the sea say to the sand?
A: Not a lot—it usually just waves.

Q: What's blue, green, yellow, purple, brown, black, and white?
A: A box of crayons.

Q: What's small and black and carries a suitcase?
A: A handle.

Q: What's a wombat for?
A: Playing wom.

Q: A man takes a barrel that weighs 20 pounds and then puts something in it. It now weighs less than 20 pounds. What did he put in the barrel?
A: A hole.

Q: What is hard to beat?
A: A broken drum.

Q: Even if you give this to someone else, you still must keep it. What is it?
A: Your word.

Q: When I point up, it's bright, but when I point down, it's dark. What am I?
A: A light switch.

Newborn babies have more than 300 bones. Adults have only 206.

WATER WORLD

It's easy to take for granted—there's so much of it. But water is one of our most precious resources.

• 70% of Earth is covered with it. From outer space, our planet looks like a blue and white sphere: the blue is water; the white is water vapor.

• Four to six gallons goes down the toilet every time you flush.

• Only 3% of the water on Earth is fresh water—the rest is salt water in the oceans.

• A 10-minute shower uses about 55 gallons of water.

• The amount of water in the Earth's environment has been virtually the same for billions of years. It doesn't increase or decrease. It just constantly goes through the *water cycle*: from ice…to liquid…to vapor…to ice…

• Turn it off! The average person uses around two gallons of water every day—just to brush their teeth.

• Two-thirds of the water used in an average home is used in the bathroom.

• When plants take water from the soil, some of it evaporates out into the air. That's called transpiration. On a hot day, a single large tree can transpire more than 50 gallons *per hour.*

• A leaky faucet can waste up to 100 gallons a day!

• Is it really a water world? Consider this fact: Scientists estimate that *95% of all living organisms* on Earth live in the oceans.

The Atlantic Ocean is saltier than the Pacific Ocean.

ALSO KNOWN AS...

Leonardo DiCaprio's agent told him to change his name to Lenny Williams so people would remember it. He refused— but these other well-known personalities all started out with different names.

WHOOPI GOLDBERG

Birth Name: Caryn Elaine Johnson

Also Known As: She was nicknamed Whoopi (as in whoopee cushion) because she farted a lot. She took the name Goldberg from the Jewish side of her family.

PINK

Birth Name: Alicia Moore

Also Known As: Pink tells several different stories about her stage name. Story #1: She took the name from the 1992 movie *Reservoir Dogs* because she resembled the Steve Buscemi character, Mr. Pink. Story #2: She turns pink whenever she is embarrassed or shy. Story #3: She picked the name because, "We're all pink on the inside."

JACKIE CHAN

Birth Name: Chan Kong-sang, which means "born in Hong Kong"

Also Known As: Chan had a co-worker on a construction site in Australia named Jack. Jack couldn't pronounce Kong-sang, so he nicknamed Chan "Little Jack." Little Jack morphed into Jackie.

Ketchup was once sold as medicine.

STING

Birth Name: Gordon Matthew Sumner

Also Known As: Bandmates nicknamed him Sting because he used to wear a yellow-and-black-striped sweater that made him look like a bee.

OPRAH WINFREY

Birth Name: Orpah Winfrey

Also Known As: Oprah Winfrey's first name is actually a typographical error on her birth certificate. Her parents wanted to name her Orpah, a biblical name, but the midwife mistakenly spelled it Oprah.

JODIE FOSTER

Birth Name: Alicia Christian Foster

Also Known As: Her brothers and sisters didn't like the name Alicia, so they called her Jodie…and it stuck.

NICOLAS CAGE

Birth Name: Nicolas Kim Coppola

Also Known As: Cage has a famous uncle, film director Francis Ford Coppola. When young Nicolas began his acting career, he wanted to make it big on his own merit, not on his famous name, so he took the last name of his favorite comic book character, Luke Cage.

Benjamin Franklin invented the rocking chair.

¡AYE CARAMBA!

Kids say the funniest things. Especially on **The Simpsons.**

"Me fail English? That's unpossible!"
—**Ralph Wiggum**

"I'm not a nerd, Bart. Nerds are smart."
—**Milhouse**

"I'm not lazy, I'm...Hey, Lisa, finish my sentence for me."
—**Bart**

"An earring, how rebellious. In a conformist sort of way."
—**Lisa**

"Dad, should I poke Rod with a sharp thing?"
—**Todd Flanders**

"The doctor said I wouldn't have so many nosebleeds if I kept my finger outta there."
—**Ralph Wiggum**

"Aren't we forgetting the true meaning of Christmas? You know, the birth of Santa."
—**Bart**

"Shoplifting is a victimless crime, like punching someone in the dark."
—**Nelson**

"Bushes are nice because they don't have prickers. Unless they do. This one did. Ouch!"
—**Ralph Wiggum**

"Remember, you can always find east by staring directly at the sun."
—**Bart**

"Why do I have the feeling that someday I'll be describing this to a psychiatrist?"
—**Lisa**

THE BALLOON FARM

You've heard of a potato farm, a wheat farm, a corn farm,
even a rutabaga farm. But how about a Balloon Farm?

BOY MEETS GIRL

Professor Carl Myers and Mary Breed Hawley were made for each
other; he liked to build hot-air balloons, and she liked to fly them.
They met and married in New York in 1871. Together, they helped
make ballooning what it is today.

UP, UP, AND AWAY

Mary's first professional flight was on July 4, 1880, in Little
Falls, New York. A crowd of 15,000 watched "Carlotta, the Lady
Aeronaut" lift off and sail east into the clouds (Mary thought
her real name was too ordinary for such an exciting career, so
she changed it to Carlotta). Once airborne, she sent four carrier
pigeons to her home in Mohawk, New York, to let her friends
know of her success. Carlotta traveled 20 miles in 35 minutes—a
triumph that launched her career as a balloonist.

A STAR IS BORN

The Myers traveled to fairs and resorts, putting on lavish balloon
shows. Dressed in a blue flannel suit, cream-colored gaiters
(leggings), and a stylish straw hat, Carlotta was always a hit
with the crowds. Audiences loved her, and the Myers made a
lot of money from their performances. But they weren't simply

Sleeping through the winter: hibernation. Through the summer? Estivation.

entertainers—they were inventors, too.

In 1889 Carlotta and the professor bought a 30-room mansion on a huge estate in Frankfort, New York, where they went to work designing and building new and better balloons. They called their new home the *Balloon Farm*.

OLD MACDONALD HAD A BALLOON

The couple made quite a team. Professor Myers specialized in building hydrogen gas balloons. He attached gigantic bags made of silk to lightweight wooden baskets wrapped in wicker. Hydrogen gas was pumped into the silk bags to inflate them. Since hydrogen is lighter than air, the balloons would lift up into the sky. Spare tanks of gas, attached to the baskets, provided more lift as needed. The couple often piloted their balloons as high as three miles above the ground! When they wanted to descend, they'd let some gas out of the bag—and down, down, down they'd come.

FIELDS OF BALLOONS

Building the balloons required acres of space...and a lot of help. While seamstresses worked in the barn—cutting and stitching together hundreds of yards of brightly colored cloth—test pilots experimented with parachutes by leaping off the roof

Scientists estimate that thoughts travel through your head at about 150 mph.

of the mansion. Workers out back stirred kettles full of bubbling varnish. In the field, yards and yards of freshly dyed balloon cloth lay draped over stakes, drying in the sun.

Visitors to the Balloon Farm (and there were thousands) described seeing the countryside dotted with the half-inflated balloons looking like gigantic pumpkins. Neighbors joked that "Farmer" Myers planted his balloon crop in the spring, gathered it in the fall, and stored it away for winter.

SKY GAMES

In the summer, there would often be a captive balloon hovering 1,200 feet above the house for research and testing purposes. The professor and his assistants used long ropes dangling from the balloon as safety belts while they flew experimental flying machines off the roof of the house.

Carlotta practiced takeoffs and landings on the front lawn in one of her homemade balloons, while Professor Myers went for afternoon sails above the house on his *Skycycle*. This flying machine was a small balloon (about half the size of a regular balloon), shaped like a football, with a bicycle-like saddle suspended from it. The professor used the pedals on the Skycycle to turn a propellor, which moved the Skycycle through the air at speeds of up to 12 miles per hour.

GONE WITH THE WIND

After completing more balloon ascents in her 10-year career than any other aeronaut, Carlotta retired from public performances in 1891. But her passion for balloons lived on through her husband. Professor Myers continued to invent: he worked with the U.S. government designing weather balloons, furnishing military balloons for use in the Spanish-American War, and even experimenting with rainmaking. His personal motto was "I refuse to let this world bore me."

The Myers sold the Balloon Farm in 1910 and moved to Atlanta, Georgia, with their daughter Ariel. But Professor Myers was still pedaling through the clouds on his Skycycle at the age of 68!

*　　*　　*

Q: What do you get when you drop all your french fries on the sofa?
A: Couch potatoes.

The Asian moon rat secretes an odor that smells like raw onions.

B**r r r r r r r r r p!**

Uncle John makes lots of phone calls, so he hears a lot of wacky answering machine greetings. Here are a few of his favorites.

• "Hi, this is the Porter residence. We're in the middle of a family fight right now. Leave your name at the beep and whoever loses will call you right back."

• "Hello. Now you say something."

• "Hi! Uncle John's answering machine is broken. This is his refrigerator. Please speak very slowly. I'll stick your message to myself with one of these magnets."

• "Hi, this is Skye and Dash's phone. If this is one of our friends, we're outside playing basketball. If this is our parents, we're at the library studying."

• "Twinkle, twinkle, little star,
  How we wonder who you are.
  Leave a message at the beep.
  We'll call back before you sleep.
  Twinkle, twinkle, little star,
  Bet you're wond'ring where we are."

• "Greetings! This is not an answering machine—this is a telepathic thought-recording device. After the tone, think about your name, your reason for calling, and a number where I can reach you, and I'll think about returning your call."

What's a squire who is also a bishop called? A *squishop*!

A KID'S CHOICE

The future of one of the best-loved books in English rested in the hands of a kid. Here's the story.

AN EXPERT OPINION

In 1936 an English book publisher named Stanley Unwin sat at his desk, staring at a manuscript. A university professor had written a children's story about the adventures of an elflike creature, and he wanted Unwin to publish it. Unwin believed that children were the best judges of children's books, so he hired his 10-year-old son, Rayner, to read the book and write a report on it.

Rayner gave it a big thumbs-up. He wrote in his report: "The book, with the help of maps, does not need illustrations. It is good and should appeal to all children between the ages of 5 and 9." His father took his advice and published it in 1937. What was the book? J.R.R. Tolkien's *The Hobbit*. It was an immediate success and has remained in print ever since.

THE STORY CONTINUES

Sixteen years later, that same kid (now grown up) was working for his father's publishing company. That's how he happened to be there when a heavy package from Professor Tolkien arrived, containing the long-awaited sequel to *The Hobbit.*

The manuscript was more than 1,000 pages long, and no one at the company thought a fantasy story that long would ever sell. Rayner Unwin thought differently. "This is a work of genius," he told his father. Then he came up with a clever idea: split the story into three parts and publish each one separately.

And that's what they did. *The Fellowship of the Ring* and *The Two Towers* were first published in 1954, and *The Return of the King* followed in 1955. The names of Bilbo, Frodo, Gandalf, Aragorn, Legolas, and Gimli went on to be known and loved by millions of readers.

And it was all because a 10-year-old boy knew a good story when he read one—and his father had the good sense to listen to his son's advice.

*   *   *

"If you can't annoy somebody, there is little point in writing."
—**Kingsley Amis**

A baseball catcher squats an average of 150 times during a nine-inning game.

MR. EAT-IT-ALL

What's the difference between a gourmet and a gourmand?
A gourmet loves to eat fine food; a gourmand just
loves to eat. Meet the world's #1 gourmand.

IRON STOMACH

Michel Lotito will eat anything. In fact, this Frenchman gets paid
to eat. His stage name is Monsieur Mangetout (pronounced,
MAWN-juh-too), which means "Mr. Eat-It-All."

Since 1966 Monsieur Mangetout's diet has included
18 bicycles, 15 shopping carts, 7 television sets,
6 chandeliers, 1 waterbed, 1 coffin (it was
empty), and a computer.

Mangetout discovered his unusual
appetite in 1959 when he was nine years
old. His friends were really impressed when
a glass broke in his mouth…and he ate it. Soon he was chowing
down on coins, nuts and bolts, plates—even razor blades! Doctors
say that his stomach lining is twice as thick as that of a normal
stomach. This allows him to consume up to two pounds of metal
per day. How does he do it? He slices everything up into little
pieces with a power saw, then swallows them whole with water—
like taking a pill.

SO WHAT'S FOR DESSERT, A CHOPPER?

Monsieur Mangetout earned a spot in the *Guinness Book of World
Records* when he ate an entire Cessna 150 airplane. That's 1,500
pounds of aluminum, steel, vinyl, Plexiglas, and rubber! It

took him two years to do it, chewing away at a rate of two pounds of aircraft a day. Monsieur Mangetout says that his stomach will digest anything his brain tells him to eat…almost. The only foods that Mr. Eat-It-All can't eat: bananas and hard-boiled eggs (they upset his stomach).

Special message from Uncle John:
Don't try this at home, kids. Remember, Monsieur Mangetout has abilities (and a stomach lining) far beyond those of normal people. Stick to your regular diet…you know, the four food groups: burgers, tacos, pizza, and cookies.

*   *   *

THE OL' SNAKE-THROUGH-THE NOSE TRICK

A 32-year-old performer named Manoharann became famous in India for a peculiar talent: he can pass a snake through his mouth and pull it out of his nostril. Other highlights of his act: he eats snakes, lizards, and cockroaches. "I learnt to do this," he explained, "because I've always been driven by the urge to do things which nobody else can."

Scientific name for winking: *nictitating.*

BITE THE WAX TADPOLE

Companies spend millions of dollars coming up with memorable campaigns to advertise their products. But crazy things can happen when those ads travel to foreign countries.

COCA-COLA

When Coca-Cola was first advertised in China, it was called *Ke-kou-ke-la.* Unfortunately, thousands of signs were printed before the Coca-Cola company discovered that the phrase meant "bite the wax tadpole" or "female horse stuffed with wax," depending on the dialect. Coca-Cola quickly renamed their product *Ko-kou-ko-le,* which can be loosely translated as "happiness in the mouth."

NIKE

Nike filmed a television commercial in Kenya using members of the Samburu tribe. As the commercial ends, the camera zooms in on a tribesman who says something in his native language. Subtitles appeared on the screen, apparently translating his words to mean the famous Nike slogan, "Just do it!"

But what the tribesman actually said was: "I don't want these. Give me bigger shoes!"

A PIRATE'S LIFE

When Uncle John was a wee lad, he dreamed of becoming a pirate, sailing the sea in search of adventure and treasure. Then he read what a pirate's life was really like...and became a writer instead. Arrrgh!

"A SHORT LIFE BUT A MERRY ONE!"

Pirates have been marauding the high seas since humans first took to the waves in ships. But the heyday of piracy was the 16th and 17th centuries, when thousands of pirates roamed the Caribbean Sea. Why there? Because of the vast fleets of Spanish treasure ships sailing back and forth from the New World to Spain, laden with gold, silver, and jewels taken from the native peoples of the Americas. These freighters, called *galleons*, were slow and clumsy, and rolled on the water like fat plums just ripe for plucking.

PRIVATEERS AND BUCCANEERS

The pirates of the Caribbean were known by many names:

Privateer. Sometimes countries actually hired pirates to raid the ships of their enemies, on the condition that these "privateers," as they were called, shared their stolen treasure, or *booty*, with the sponsoring government. Many pirates started out as privateers... but then decided to work for themselves. The most successful of them was Sir Henry Morgan (see page 110), who later became lieutenant governor of Jamaica.

Buccaneer. The word is taken from the French word boucanier, which means "one who hunts wild pigs." It was the name given to the drifters, rogues, and deserters who lived together in bands on deserted islands off Jamaica or Cuba. Many of them eventually grew tired of hunting pigs and went after richer game on the seas. Their name followed them.

Marooner. This name comes from the old Spanish word *cimarrón*, which means "deserter" or "runaway." Many pirates started out as sailors in European navies but deserted as soon as they could. Some pirates were African slaves brought to the New World to work for the Spanish. Those who escaped and joined the pirate bands became known as *cimarrónes negros.*

...WELL, MAYBE NOT SO MERRY

It was a rare pirate who lived to old age. Most were dead within two years of turning pirate—usually by execution. So why do it? Because in those days, the life of a regular sailor was brutal. Many sailors were *impressed* into service, which means they were captured and forced to become sailors. Routinely beaten by officers, paid poorly, and at sea for months at a time, many sailors deserted at the first port of call.

These tough, hardened men had been trained to sail and fight. For many of them, the life of a pirate with its adventure and plunder was their best option and their only chance for a taste of freedom.

COMPUTER SPEAK

Ever wonder where names like Google and Hotmail come from? Here are the answers.

APPLE. What's the favorite fruit of Apple Computer founder Steve Jobs? Apples, of course. In 1976 the new company was three months late filing an official name and Jobs just wanted to get it done. He told his colleagues that if they didn't come up with a name he liked by five o'clock, he was naming the company Apple. They didn't, so he did.

ADOBE. In 1982 John Warnock named this computer software giant after Adobe Creek which ran behind his house in Los Altos, California.

GOOGLE. In 1998 Sergey Brin and Larry Page were looking for money to help start their company, so they boasted to investors that their new search engine could find a googol pieces of information, which is the word for the numeral "1" followed by 100 zeroes. One investor liked their pitch, and immediately wrote a check made out to "Google." The name stuck.

HOTMAIL. In 1995 Jack Smith came up with a program to access e-mail from anywhere in the world. His partner, Sabeer Bhatia, wanted to use the word "mail" in the program's name and tried to find a word to go with it. He finally chose "Hotmail" because it uses the letters "html" in the word, which is the programming language used to write Web pages. It was originally written as: "HoTMaiL."

It takes 12 drawings to make one second of motion in an animated cartoon.

HP. When Bill Hewlett and Dave Packard founded their electronics company in 1939, they tossed a coin to decide whether it would be called Packard-Hewlett or Hewlett-Packard. Bill won.

JAVA. Originally James Gosling called his programming language "Oak," after a tree that stood outside his window. But someone was already using that name, so in 1992 his programming team picked "Java," after their favorite drink—coffee.

MICROSOFT. In 1975 Bill Gates and Paul Allen created a company dedicated to building microcomputer software. Gates took the first half of each word and named the company Micro-Soft. He later dropped the hyphen between the two words.

MOTOROLA. Today Motorola makes microchips, but back in the 1930s, Paul Galvin's company made car radios. Victrola was the most popular manufacturer of phonographs, so Galvin added *motor* to the *ola* and came up with "Motorola" as a way of saying "sound in motion."

YAHOO! Author Jonathan Swift first used the word *yahoo* over 250 years ago in his famous book, *Gulliver's Travels*. It means a person who is rude and repulsive in appearance and action. In 1994 Jerry Yang and David Filo chose that name for their popular Internet gateway because they considered themselves to be major yahoos.

IN THE FUTURE...

People keep coming up with ways to make things easier and easier—and we're not done yet!

DIRTY DISHES

Today's Problem: Your mom says, "Wash the dishes," but you've just learned in science class that every family needs to learn how to conserve water and energy.

Tomorrow's Solution: Clean those dishes with sound-waves! No water, no soap, no heat, no drying—and it only takes a minute. Ultrasonic cleaning machines use sound frequencies that are too high for humans to hear—but they're just the right frequency to knock dirt off dishes with sonic vibrations. We already have machines that combine ultrasonic frequencies with water to clean airplane parts, jewelry, and teeth (you might even have an ultrasonic toothbrush in your bathroom). Engineers still have to figure out a way to do it without using water, but once they do, ultrasonic dish cleaning will have arrived.

LONG LINES

Today's Problem: You and your dad want to get in and out of the grocery store quickly. But even the express checkout line is backed up all the way down the aisle. You're stuck—*argh!*

Tomorrow's Solution: Soon you'll be able to shop till you drop and never have to wait in line. The same E-Z Pass technology that lets a car skip through a tollbooth on a bridge or highway is coming to a store near you. A scanner will read the prices of all of your groceries as you push your cart through the checkout and

Shrek's name came from the German word *schreck*, which means "scariness."

automatically charge your credit card. And you'll be out of there before you know it!

SMART SNEAKERS

Today's Problem: You're out shooting hoops with your friends. You fake right and drive for the basket and—*ouch*—you twist your ankle.

Tomorrow's Solution: Smart sneakers! The research people at Nike and Reebok say they'll soon have shoes that respond to each person's unique stride, jump, step, and hop. By sensing your movements with an imbedded computer chip, the sneakers will instantly mold their shape to your foot. No more twisted ankles. No more tweaked knees. Bonus: These smart sneakers will also be able to tell your coach just how far and how fast you ran. (No more faking it!)

LAND-SEA ROVER

Today's Problem: Your family wants to go waterskiing, but first you have to hitch your boat to the car, drive to a lake, unload the boat, gas it up, and then find a parking spot. By the time you get in the water, half your day's gone.

Tomorrow's Solution: Researchers at Gibbs Technology in England are testing a new sports car that drives on the water as well as on land. They call it the Aquada. On land it can zoom along at 100 miles per hour. Want to hit the water? Flip a switch—the wheels retract, the jet propulsion system kicks in, and it zips around at 30 mph. *Yee-haw!*

WACKY HOLIDAYS

If you don't mind people thinking you're a bit weird, you can celebrate all year long!

January 3: Drinking Straw Day

January 16: National Nothing Day

January 21: Squirrel Appreciation Day

February 15: National I Want Butterscotch Day

February 20: "Hoodie-Hoo!" Day

March 15: Act Happy Day

April 10: National Siblings Day

May 1: Mother Goose Day

May 3: Lumpy Rug Day

June 19: Join Hands Day

July 3: Compliment Your Mirror Day

July 7: Father-Daughter Take a Walk Together Day

July 19: Cow Appreciation Day

July 27: Take Your Houseplant for a Walk Day

August 7: Mustard Day

August 10: National S'Mores Day

September 19: Talk Like a Pirate Day (*Aarrrgh!*)

September 22: Elephant Appreciation Day

October 6: Mad Hatter Day

October 31: National Knock-Knock Day

November 26: Buy Nothing Day

December 11: Day of the Horse

December 16: Chocolate-Covered Everything Day

When astronauts sleep, their arms float out in front of their bodies.

SECRET MESSAGE

Want to write notes that your parents and teachers can't read? Of course you do. Here's how.

CREATING A CODE

A *St. Cyr Cipher slide* (named after the French military academy where it was invented in the 1800s) is an easy-to-make coding and decoding device. It is made from two pieces of paper. The first piece is called "the mask." It has two slits at each end and has the alphabet printed on it once. The second piece of paper is called "the strip." The strip is longer than the mask and has the alphabet printed twice on it.

To work the slide, you pull the strip through the mask so that the letters on it align with different letters on the mask. For example, in the diagram below, A=E, B=F, D=H, and so on.

Supplies: paper, scissors, ruler, and pen or pencil

Instructions:

1. Cut a piece of paper 2 inches wide and 6 inches long. About ½ inch from each end, cut 2 vertical slits a little more than ½ inch long (see diagram). This is the mask.

The smell of minty toothpaste can attract bears.

2. At the top of the mask above the strip and between the slits, write the alphabet, spacing the letters evenly apart as shown.

3. Cut another piece of paper slightly less than ½ inch wide and 11 inches long. This is the strip.

4. Write the alphabet on the strip two times in a row.

5. Slip the strip into the mask.

6. Now you can create your own secret message! First, write your real message on a sheet of paper.

7. To encode your message, pick a letter on the mask (any letter) and slide the strip to line up the first letter in your message under it. These two letters are now "the key." Without moving the strip, encode your message by switching the real letters in your message to the letters on the mask one by one, and writing them down.

8. To decipher a message, just reverse the process.

Use the picture on the previous page to decipher this important message:

OMHW VYPI, EHYPXW HVSSP!

What does it say? For the answer, turn to page 284.

GULLFRIENDS

*Seagulls, it seems, have personalities. They can be
nice and friendly...or mean and vindictive!*

GOOD GULL

Eighty-two-year-old Rachel Flynn lived with her sister June on
the rugged coast of Cape Cod, Massachusetts. They made a habit
of feeding a seagull that came to their house every day. Eventually
they became so attached to the bird that they named it Nancy.

One day in 1980, while Rachel was taking her usual walk along
the high cliffs near their home, she slipped off the edge of the path
and fell 32 feet onto an isolated beach below. Because she had
fallen between two boulders, she couldn't move. Rachel was certain
no one would find her...and that she would die there.

To the Rescue!

Just when Rachel was about to give up hope, she spied a seagull
circling above her. Could it possibly be her gull? Rachel cried out,
"For God's sake, Nancy, get help!" and the seagull flew off.

A mile away, June was working in the kitchen when she heard
an insistent tapping at her window. Looking outside, she saw the
gull flapping its wings frantically and "making more noise than a
wild turkey."

June tried to shoo the bird away, but Nancy kept up the racket,
flapping and pecking at the windowpane for 15 minutes. Finally,
June decided that the bird must be trying to tell her something.
She went outside and watched the seagull fly off toward the beach,
then come back to June, as if saying, "Follow me." So she did.

Ants and cockroaches can dodge the rays in a microwave oven and survive.

Nancy led June straight to the edge of the cliff. June peered over the edge, saw her sister lying helpless below, and immediately ran back to call the rescue squad. Rachel was saved, and Nancy the seagull was declared a hero!

BAD GULL

In June 1994, Don Weston of Gloucester, England, heard a young seagull squawking in his driveway. He took pity on the little bird and set it on the roof of his house to keep it safe from cats and dogs. A few hours later, it flew away.

Weston thought the seagull would be grateful that he'd saved its life, but the bird seems to feel quite the opposite. Every June, the angry seagull comes back to torment Weston. Every time the bird catches sight of him, it goes berserk. It dive-bombs him, pecks at his head, and poops on him. It has even stalked him through the city by air.

Weston knows it's the same gull because he recognizes its distinctive squawking. He says it sounds "like a banshee wailing." He has nightmares about the demon bird and dreads the coming of June. The really bad news: Seagulls can live for 25 years.

Who wood know? A two-by-four actually measures 1 ½ by 3 ½ inches.

NAMED AFTER A KID

Wouldn't it be cool to have something named after you? You would be famous forever!

A DOLL

This famous doll was named after a real girl. Her name was Barbara, and she was the daughter of Ruth and Elliot Handler, who owned the Mattel Toy Company. Mrs. Handler noticed that her preteen daughter, Barbara, had lost interest in baby dolls. Instead she was cutting out pictures of young women in magazines and pasting clothes on them. So Mrs. Handler invented a new kind of doll and called it—you guessed it—*Barbie*. Mattel introduced the Barbie doll in 1959, and since then it's become the most popular doll of all time. More than 500 million have been sold. In fact, three Barbie dolls are sold every second of the day!

A CARTOON CHARACTER

In 1947 cartoonist Hank Ketcham and his wife, Alice, welcomed their bouncing baby boy into the world and named him Dennis. From the beginning, Dennis was a rambunctious kid. By age four, Ketcham said Dennis was "too young for school, too big for his playpen, too small to hit, not old enough for jail—and 100% anti-establishment." One day during his supposed nap, little Dennis tore apart his bedroom. Then, to make matters worse, he spread peanut butter and the contents of a loaded diaper all over the room. Alice Ketcham told her husband, "Your son is a menace!"

Mrs. Ketcham's comment inspired her husband to draw a proposal for a one-panel comic strip about a loveable boy who was full of mischief. He named it *Dennis the Menace*. The comic strip debuted March 12, 1951, and by the end of the year, *Dennis the Menace* was a feature in 100 newspapers around the country. Since that star-studded beginning, *Dennis the Menace* has been turned into a book series, a cartoon, two live-action TV series, and several movies.

A COMPUTER

In January 1983, Apple Computer introduced a personal computer that had cost $50 million to develop. It was the first personal computer to use a GUI (Graphical User Interface), which allowed the user to create pictures. It was also the first personal computer to use a mouse. The price tag was a whopping $10,000—very expensive at any time. It was called Lisa, which officially stood for Local Integrated Software Architecture. Unofficially, Lisa just happened to be the name of the daughter of Apple Computer founder Steve Jobs. Little Lisa Jobs was born in 1978. Lisa the computer entered the world five years later.

GASSY POETRY

*Not one, not two, but three fine blasts of
classic gas from the poetical past.*

ODE TO BEANS

Beans, beans, the musical fruit!
The more you eat, the more you toot.
The more you toot, the better you feel,
So let's have beans for every meal!

Beans, beans, they're good for the heart!
The more you eat, the more you fart.
The more you fart, the better you feel,
So let's have beans for every meal!

DR. BART'S FARTS

There once was a doctor named Bart
Who told all his patients to fart.
He said the relief
Was usually brief
But terribly good for the heart.

R.I.P.

(*found on a tombstone in Stanley, Tasmania*)
Wherever you may be
O let your wind go free
'Cos holding it caused the death of me.

Myth-nomer: Black-eyed peas are actually beans.

GHOSTS IN THE WHITE HOUSE

At the end of a president's term, he (and his family) are
supposed to move out of the White House. Well, not all of the
occupants of the White House want to move. Some prefer
to stick around, pacing the halls, knocking on doors,
staring out windows…or just hanging up laundry.

ABIGAIL ADAMS (died 1818)

Abigail Adams, wife of President John Adams, is the oldest ghost
to be spotted wandering the halls of the White House. She is
usually seen hurrying to the East Room with her arms outstretched
as if she's carrying a load of laundry. She's going to that room
because when she was first lady, the White House wasn't yet
completed. Many of the rooms were freezing cold and damp. One
of the warmest spots in the house was the East Room, which is
where Mrs. Adams hung her clothes to dry.

DOLLEY MADISON (died 1849)

Dolley Madison prided herself on the rose garden that she planted
when her husband, James Madison, was president. Later, in 1918,
President Woodrow Wilson's wife, Edith, decided to have the roses
dug up so she could plant her own garden. According to legend,
Mrs. Madison's ghost appeared and yelled at the gardener. She
ordered him not to touch a thing—and he didn't! Mrs. Wilson
decided to find another spot for her flowers, and Mrs. Madison's
rose garden continues to bloom to this day.

ANDREW JACKSON (died 1845)

The ghost of Andrew Jackson spends his time near the Rose Room, where his bed is on display. Mary Todd Lincoln reported hearing him pacing up and down the halls, cursing. Others have heard him laughing inside the Rose Room.

ABRAHAM LINCOLN (died 1865)

Abraham Lincoln is the ghost most often seen in the White House. President Calvin Coolidge's wife, Grace, was the first to spot him. She said he was standing at the window of the Oval Office with his hands clasped behind his back, gazing out at the Potomac River.

• Queen Wilhelmina of the Netherlands was a guest of the White House when she heard a knock in the middle of the night. She opened the door and there stood Lincoln wearing his famous top hat. The queen fainted. When she awoke, he was gone.

• Eleanor Roosevelt's secretary, Mary Eben, reported seeing Lincoln sitting on the bed in the Lincoln Room, pulling on his boots. Many other people have reported seeing him lying on the bed.

• And speaking of Lincoln, every April on the anniversary of his assassination, legend has it that a ghostly train travels along the tracks between Washington, D.C., and Illinois. This phantom is the funeral train that took Lincoln's body back home to Illinois, where he was buried.

MR. BURNS (date of death...unknown)

The most unusual ghost in the White House is a man named David Burns. In 1790 he donated the land for the White House. Over the subsequent years, many people have heard him call their name. When they turn to see who called, the ghost always introduces himself, "I'm Mr. Burns."

*　　*　　*

"Leave nothing for tomorrow which can be done today."

—**Abraham Lincoln**

Q: How does the tailor bird get its name? A: Using its beak as a needle...

MERMAID TALES

Most people write them off as just another fish story. But you never know—mermaids might be as real as Bigfoot.

A FISH BY ANY OTHER NAME

To the Irish she's a *merrow*. The Greeks call her a *siren*. Her Japanese name is *ningyo*. The Inuit people of Canada know her as *nuyagpalik*. But most of us know her as a *mermaid*. Half-human, half-fish, mermaids are found in the folklore of almost every country in the world. For thousands of years, people have claimed to see them swimming in the Mediterranean Sea, off the reefs of New Zealand, and between the ice floes of Alaska. Even Christopher Columbus said he saw mermaids swimming in the Atlantic as he sailed to the New World.

A BIG SPLASH IN HISTORY

The Roman historian Pliny the Elder (23–79 A.D.) reported the mermaids in the Gulf of Cádiz off the coast of Spain. Pliny's word was so respected that hundreds of years later, the people of the Middle Ages believed mermaids existed simply because he said so.

In ancient times, no one was too anxious to see one. The mermaid's beautiful singing was said to have hypnotized many a sailor and, like the sounds of the Sirens in Greek mythology, lured them to wreck their ships on dangerous rocks. Superstitious sailors tossed gold coins or poured wine into the water, hoping to bribe mermaids into leaving them alone during rough crossings.

...and plant fibers for thread, it sews two leaves together to make its nest.

CLOSE ENCOUNTERS

Public fascination with mermaids peaked in the 1800s. Lots of fakes were displayed at fairs and exhibitions. P.T. Barnum put a "mermaid mummy" on view in his circus sideshow. His "Feejee Mermaid"—with the bodies of a fish, a baby orangutan, and a monkey head all stitched together—quickly became a star attraction.

But have there been any *real* mermaid sightings? Here are a few firsthand accounts:

• In 1608 the navigator and explorer Henry Hudson reported that his crew had spotted a mermaid swimming close by the side of their ship. He wrote in his ship's log: "From the navel upward, her back and breasts were like a woman's; her skin was very white with long hair hanging down. They saw her tail, which was like the tail of a porpoise and speckled like a mackerel."

• On September 8, 1809, *The Times* of London published a letter from a schoolmaster in Sandside Bay, Scotland. William Munro described watching a mermaid sitting on a rock combing her hair: "The creature appeared to be an unclothed female with long, flowing light brown hair and blue eyes. She seemed to be a fully grown human, with normal mouth and nose, and though I can't be certain, her fingers did not appear to be webbed." Munro said he watched the mermaid for three or four minutes until she dropped back into the sea.

• Around 1830 the people of Benbecula Island in the Scottish Hebrides claimed to have seen a mermaid playing in the sea.

George Washington soaked his false teeth in wine to improve their taste.

Some men tried to swim out and capture her, but she easily swam out of their reach. When a boy threw a rock and hit her, she swam away. A few days later, her body reportedly washed ashore about two miles away. Crowds gathered at the beach to see her. After the corpse had been examined, Sheriff Duncan Shaw ordered a coffin made, after which she was buried on the shore.

MORE MERMAID SIGHTINGS

• In 1947 a fisherman from the Hebrides island of Muck saw a mermaid sitting on a floating herring box (used to preserve live lobsters), combing her hair. She dove into the sea as soon as she saw him. To his death in the 1950s, the man remained convinced that he had seen a real mermaid.

Gold never tarnishes or corrodes—it stays bright forever.

• On December 20, 1977, the *Pretoria News* of South Africa reported that a mermaid was found in a storm sewer in the township of Lusaka. She was first seen by children. A reporter was told that the creature appeared to be a "European woman from the waist up, whilst the rest of her body was shaped like the back end of a fish, and covered with scales."

• In 1978 a 41-year-old Filipino fisherman named Jacinto Fatalvero claimed not only that he saw a mermaid one moonlit night but also that she helped him net his fish.

FISH TALES

Do mermaids really exist? Today most experts feel these sightings are of seals or manatees that have been mistaken for mermaids. Yet others find it hard to ignore the detailed reports of Columbus, Hudson, and others. So is the mermaid a fish…or just fishy? You decide.

Blowhard: There are more than 10,000 geysers at Yellowstone National Park.

LUCKY #7

*In almost every culture, seven is considered a lucky
number. We're not superstitious, but we put this
on page 77 because...well...you never know.*

PERFECT NUMBER

• Seven has been thought to be a magical number for thousands
of years. Ancient people considered it the number that governs the
rhythm of life. Their lives revolved around the phases of the moon,
which has four cycles of 7 days.

• Among the Sumerians, Babylonians, and Egyptians, there were 7
sacred planets: the sun, moon, Mercury, Venus, Mars, Jupiter, and
Saturn.

• The Sumerians named their gods after these 7 planets and were
the first to divide the week into 7 days, each ruled by a god. So did
the Romans, the Celts, and the Germanic and Norse peoples of
Europe.

• The ancient Greeks called 7 the perfect number, as it was the
sum of the triangle (3) and the square (4), which they considered
perfect mathematical figures.

• Seven appears in the Bible more times than any other number.
For instance, God created the Earth in six days, and then rested on
the 7th day. Joshua brought down the walls of Jericho by circling
the city 7 times.

• In China, the 7th day of the first moon of the lunar year is called
Human's Day. The Chinese mark this day as the birthday of all
human beings.

The original 7-Up recipe contained horseradish.

OOP DREAMS

Football, baseball, and basketball—the big three American sports. But did you know that basketball was invented by a Canadian? Here's the story.

WINTER BALL

In the winter of 1891, YMCA sports instructor James Naismith had a problem. It was his job to provide the local boys of Springfield, Massachusetts, with healthy activities all year-round. They played football in the fall, baseball in spring and summer—but winter was a big blank. The Canadian-born Naismith tried indoor soccer, but dropped it when it led to a broken leg and some broken windows. Indoor lacrosse was no better—these field games needed more room than a gymnasium could provide.

PEACHY!

So Naismith invented a new game. On December 21, 1891, he hung a peach basket from the overhead balcony at each end of the gym. He split his 18 kids into two teams and held up a soccer ball. The object of his new game? To toss the ball into the opponent's peach basket while keeping the other team from tossing it into yours. With that, the game of basketball was born!

Within a year, the new game had spread to

other YMCAs, then to colleges and athletic clubs. But basketball was different back then, and it would take some time before it evolved into the sport we know today.

MAKING AND BREAKING THE RULES

At first the game was all about passing: If a player had the ball, he couldn't run with it—he had to pass or shoot. Players quickly got past that rule by juggling the ball up in the air as they ran. Technically, they were "passing" the ball to themselves. This became known as traveling and was made illegal.

The players didn't like the new rule and took matters into their own hands—literally. They bounced the ball with two hands and ran between the bounces. This was called *double dribbling*, and a rule against it was made in 1898. The rule makers figured that would put an end to the practice, because no one thought players would ever master one-handed dribbling.

They were wrong. Dribbling with one hand quickly became the players' favorite way to move the ball downcourt. Rule makers finally gave in to player pressure, and by 1910 players were given permission to dribble the ball. Until 1916, for some reason, a dribbler wasn't allowed to shoot—he had to pass the ball to another player, who could then shoot.

WHERE'S THE BALL?

In the early days, everybody on a team got to play—at the same time. As many as 50 players might play on each side. When fans started complaining that they couldn't see the ball with so many players on the court, teams quickly scaled back, experimenting

Geese: On the ground, they're called a *gaggle*. In the air, they're a *skein*.

with smaller squads. The first game with five players on each side was in 1896 between the University of Chicago and the University of Iowa. Within a year, nearly every college team in the country had switched to five-man teams.

HOME COURT ADVANTAGE

The backboard was invented in 1895 to keep fans from reaching over the balconies where the baskets were hung and "helping" a player's shot find the hoop. Loyal fans weren't afraid to help their team in other ways, too. They'd throw stuff at opposing players and even reach out and trip them with umbrellas. Soon the games had to be played inside net cages to protect the players. (Basketball players came to be known as "cagers," a nickname that stuck around long after the net cages were gone.)

In less than a century, basketball has grown to become, after soccer, the world's most popular sport. According to the International Federation of Basketball, more than 400 million people play it—1 out of every 12 people on Earth!

*　　*　　*

AN AMAZING RECORD

Longest Basketball Game: A game between Australian amateur league teams, the Suncoast Clippers and the Marochydore Eagles, lasted 24 hours—from November 21, 1998 to November 22, 1998.

Scared of clowns? You're a *coulrophobe*. (But so is actor Johnny Depp.)

WHY WE SAY IT

*Here's the inside scoop on some words
and phrases we use every day.*

YOU'RE FIRED!

Meaning: An exclamation an angry boss might use to let an employee know he's out of a job

Origin: Hundreds of years ago, when clans in Scotland wanted to get rid of unwelcome neighbors without killing them, they burned their houses down—hence the expression "to get fired."

COMPUTER BUG

Meaning: A problem in the computer's software

Origin: In 1945 a computer at Harvard University malfunctioned. Grace Hopper, who was working on the computer, investigated and found a moth in one of the circuits. Ever since, when something goes wrong with a computer it is said to "have a bug in it."

BOO

Meaning: An exclamation used to frighten or surprise someone

Origin: In Norse mythology, Boh was the name of a great general who was the son of the god Odin. The very mention of his name panicked his enemies. Boh eventually became a word used to frighten children. *Boo!*

"Mare's tails" and "cat's paws" are both types of clouds.

TOP DRAWER

Meaning: The best quality

Origin: Traditionally, the top drawer of a dresser in British and American households was the place where jewelry and other valuables are kept.

TO BE BESIDE YOURSELF

Meaning: To be under great emotional stress.

Origin: The ancient Greeks believed that when a person was under intense pressure, the soul left the body and "was beside itself."

SO LONG

Meaning: Good-bye

Origin: English sailors who came back from the Middle East liked to use the Arabic word for good-bye: *salaam*. But the way it came out of their mouths sounded more like "so long," and that's the way this phrase entered the English language.

TO BARK UP THE WRONG TREE

Meaning: When you try to solve a problem by using the wrong method

Origin: Hunters have used dogs to track animals for thousands of years. Some dogs have been trained to chase their prey to a tree and then bark at that tree. But dogs sometimes get confused and make mistakes. When this happens, the hunter arrives to find no animal up there. The dog is, literally, barking up the wrong tree.

There are at least 200 different shapes of pasta.

WEIRD JOBS

When Uncle John was a kid he wanted to be a pirate.
Somehow he ended up making **Bathroom Readers.**
Hey, it's better than sniffing armpits.

ARMPIT SNIFFER

Betty Lyons is a *scent technician* (sometimes also called an *odor judge*) for Cincinnati Hilltop Labs in Ohio. She tests smells for a living. People who do this can identify thousands of different odors at up to 20 levels of intensity. Presented with a new scent, an odor judge can list what's in it and how much of it is there, which is very useful when a company wants to analyze a competitor's product.

According to the book *Odd Jobs*, by Nancy Schiff, Lyons's main job is to help companies test deodorants. She spends her days smelling diapers, cat litter, shoes, and armpits to make sure each kind of deodorant works. Betty doesn't put her nose directly in the armpit or diaper. She keeps a safe distance from the things she smells by placing a paper tube between her nose and the offending object.

When it comes to body odors, she says, "Everything you eat—fried chicken, alcohol, pickles—comes out under your arm. It comes out anyplace you sweat, even on your feet."

Think you've got a nose for this job? Want to be a before-and-after armpit and foot sniffer? Go for it! Good ones earn $40,000 to $50,000 a year.

***Spelunking* is the sport of exploring caves.**

ROAD KILL REMOVER

You've probably never thought about it, but when animals are hit by cars on highways, someone has to take them away. People called *road kill removers* (RKRs) are hired to do the job. Most of the bodies are dumped in landfills, but not all. Workers in this business—sometimes called *pet wranglers*— are allowed to keep all the

hides they can salvage. There are other benefits, too, says one RKR. "You can cook all you can scrape up, so it cuts down on grocery bills." Typical pay for this job: $30,000 a year—and all you can eat.

GLASS EYE PAINTER

Why do glass eyes look so real? An artist paints them that way. Annette Kirszrot owns her own artificial eye business in New York. She's been painting prosthetic eyes for more than 30 years. She has painted thousands of them and says, "No two eyes are ever alike." By the way, most glass eyes made in the United States aren't glass at all—they're made of plastic!

Molly Pitchers were women who carried pitchers of water onto battlefields...

ICE CREAM TASTER

Wow! A job where you eat ice cream all day! Sounds like a dream, doesn't it? According to ice cream taster John Harrison, it's not quite what you think—he doesn't really eat the ice cream he tastes. Using a gold-plated spoon (to make sure he tastes only the ice cream's flavor), he first swirls the ice cream in his mouth to cover all 10,000 taste buds on his tongue. Then he smacks his lips to bring in room-temperature air. Meanwhile he's checking to see if the ice cream is smooth and creamy. If it's icy, gummy, or coarse, he gives it a thumbs-down. Then, after he's swirled, smacked, and rated his ice cream, he spits it out into a trash barrel. His favorite flavor: cookies and cream (he invented it).

*   *   *

LOONEY LAWS

- In Newark, New Jersey, it's illegal to sell ice cream after 6 p.m....unless the customer has a note from a doctor.
- If a frog's croaking keeps you awake in Memphis, Tennessee, you can have it arrested.
- And don't even think about letting your sheep run wild in the schoolyard if you live in Vermont: It's totally illegal.

...to cool off the cannons during the American Revolution.

CELL PHONE TAG

Things have changed a lot since Uncle John was a kid...like, when did "tag" go digital?

OBJECT OF THE GAME: To be the team that tags the most people

NUMBER OF PLAYERS: As many kids as possible—the more the better

SETUP: Divide the group into teams of 2 to 3 players. Each team needs a cell phone, a sheet of paper, and a pencil. Exchange team phone numbers and program them into speed dial. Agree on a home base, then decide how long you want the game to last. Next, set boundaries for the playing field (mall, park, neighborhood, etc.).

HOW TO PLAY: To start, teams go and hide. You are on the prowl to spot the other teams and tag them—without being seen! When you see another team, "tag" them by calling their cell phone. You must speak to the team directly (no voice messages) and describe exactly where they're hiding. If the other team sees you, the tag doesn't count and they must give you 2 minutes to rehide before they can tag you back. Record your tags and the locations on your sheet of paper. Continue tagging (and avoiding being tagged) until the time is up.

At the end of the game, meet back at home base. The team with the most tags wins. Bonus: It's free on weekends!

CLASSICAL KOOK

Most of us know that Beethoven was a great composer—maybe the greatest who has ever lived. Here are some facts you may not know about this eccentric musical genius.

LUDWIG VAN BEETHOVEN

Born: Bonn, Germany, 1770
Died: Vienna, Austria, 1827

• He had a rare condition called *synesthesia*, which means the senses are connected: for example, a person can taste sounds, and musical notes are seen in colors.

• He was only 26 and at the height of his career when his hearing began to fail. The condition grew worse until, at age 47, he was completely deaf. Amazingly, he wrote some of his greatest works—including his Ninth Symphony ("Ode to Joy")—after this point.

• Beethoven never washed his clothes. His friends would take them while he slept, and replace them with clean ones. Beethoven never noticed.

• His buck teeth were the cleanest part of his body because he rubbed them constantly with a napkin.

• Beethoven was known for spitting in restaurants and dumping plates of food on people's heads.

• His favorite foods were macaroni and cheese, red herrings, egg and bread soup, and extra-strong coffee.

• Once he got angry at a prince who was supporting him and said, "There are thousands of princes. There is only one Beethoven!" (Of course, he was right.)

In a hurry? A grand piano can be played faster than an upright piano.

ASK THE EXPERTS

Uncle John asks a lot of questions. And when he needs an answer, where does he go? To the experts.

BAD BREATH

Q: *What causes bad breath?*

A: There are two possible causes for bad breath: The first is a problem called *halitosis*, which is a result of not brushing your teeth, tooth decay, or gum diseases. To solve this problem you need to brush regularly or be treated by a dentist or periodontist (a doctor who treats gum disease). The other cause could be the food you eat. Onions and garlic contain oils that are absorbed by the digestive system and passed on to the bloodstream. Then the blood transports the oils to the lungs. In the lungs, the oils mix with the carbon dioxide gas that you just naturally exhale and that produces bad-smelling breath. (From *Icky Squishy Science*, by Sandra Markle)

RED EYE

Q: *Why do eyes sometimes come out red in photographs?*

A: The flash from the camera is being reflected on the rear of the eyeball, which is red from all the blood vessels. So how do you stop that? Use a flash that is not attached to the camera or get your subjects to look somewhere else. Another trick is to turn up the lights in the room, making them as bright as possible, which will

According to zoologists, sheep are the dumbest animals in the world.

cause the subject's pupils to contract and admit less of the light from the flash. (From *Why Things Are*, by Joel Achenbach)

FRECKLES

Q: *What causes freckles?*

A: Unless you're albino, your skin has cells called *melanocytes*, which produce melanin, a dark pigment that absorbs ultraviolet light. When your skin is exposed to sunlight, these cells make melanin at a faster rate, which is why you get a suntan.

All melanocytes are not created equal—some are more active than others. Result: When groups of very active melanocytes are surrounded by less active melanocytes, you get little islands of color...known as "freckles." (From *Can Elephants Swim?*, by Robert Jones)

ICE SCREAM

Q: *What causes an ice cream headache?*

A: When you eat ice cream or drink really cold water, the second that cold touches the roof of your mouth, the nerves in your palate send out an alert causing the blood vessels in your head to instantly swell up. The swollen blood vessels act like a vise grip on your head and give you that instant headache.

Want to stop the pain? Try pressing your tongue to the top of your mouth to warm up your palate. (From *Oh, Yuck: The Encyclopedia of Everything Nasty*, by Joy Masoff)

WISE WORDS

Some wise quotes from some wise folks.

"We should not let our fears hold us back from pursuing our hopes."
—**John F. Kennedy**

"The best and most beautiful things in the world cannot be seen or even touched. They must be felt with the heart."
—**Helen Keller**

"When we care more about the future of our children than on avenging the past, there is hope for peace."
—**Madeleine Albright**

"If you run into a wall, don't turn around and give up. Figure out how to climb it, go through it, or work around it."
—**Michael Jordan**

"If you want others to be happy, practice compassion. If you want to be happy, practice compassion."
—**The Dalai Lama**

"Honesty is the first chapter in the book of wisdom."
—**Thomas Jefferson**

"Doing the best at this moment puts you in the best place for the next moment."
—**Oprah Winfrey**

"Live as if you were to die tomorrow. Learn as if you were to live forever."
—**Mahatma Gandhi**

"Joy is not in things! It is in us!"
—**Benjamin Franklin**

Calendar rule: Any month that starts on a Sunday will have a Friday the 13th.

WILD KIDS

You've heard of Tarzan the Ape Man, and Mowgli, the boy who was raised by wolves in The Jungle Book. *But did you know there are real kids who have been raised by animals?*

GAZELLE GUY

In 1960 Jean-Claude Armen went into the Spanish Sahara in search of a wild child who lived with a herd of gazelles. Natives pointed him to the place where the boy had been seen, and sure enough, Armen found him "galloping in gigantic bounds among a long cavalcade of white gazelles."

The boy, who was about 10, walked on all fours, pulled up desert roots with his teeth, and constantly twitched his muscles, ears, and nose like the rest of the herd. He had thick muscular ankles from leaping and running. Armen observed that the boy had even learned to speak the gazelle "language": He would stamp to indicate the distance of a food source and greet the other gazelles by sniffing and licking them.

Running Like the Wind

Armen chased the boy with a Jeep to see how fast he could run and was astonished to discover the boy hit speeds of 32 miles per hour. (Olympic sprinters can only reach about 25 miles per hour in short bursts.)

Though several people tried, the gazelle boy was never captured. He may still be out there in the Spanish Sahara, leaping and running with the gazelles.

Pumice is the only rock that floats in water.

MONKEY BOY

When John Ssabanya was only two, he was abandoned in the dense jungle of Uganda and left to die. Luckily for John, some monkeys found him and adopted him as part of their family. For the next four years, John climbed trees and hunted for fruit, nuts, and berries, just like a monkey.

In 1991 a woman out gathering firewood spotted the naked boy with his monkey family and told the people in her village. When they tried to catch John, he ran up a tree and hurled sticks at them. His monkey parents put up a ferocious fight to protect him. But he was finally caught and later adopted by Paul and Molly Wasswa, who run the Kamuzinda Christian Orphanage in Masaka.

Straightening Up

It took John nine years to learn to speak and to stand up straight like a human. He still has an odd, lopsided walk, and when he smiles, he pulls his lips back just like a monkey. John greets people with a powerful hug, which is the way monkeys say hello. When he was taken to visit monkeys, he avoided eye contact and approached them from the side with open palms, just as he'd been taught to do by his monkey parents.

Now in his teens, John still speaks a little slowly, but he has a big singing voice and is a member of the Pearl of Africa Children's Choir.

An ostrich's eye is bigger than its brain.

WOLF GIRLS

Near Godamuri, India, villagers found two little girls living in a giant anthill with their adopted family—a pack of wolves. The mother wolf fought hard to protect her two "cubs," but villagers killed the she-wolf, took the girls, and gave them to Reverend Singh, a Christian missionary.

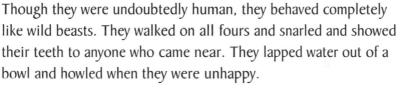

The girls were named Kamala and Amala. Kamala appeared to be about eight years old, and Amala was not quite two. Though they were undoubtedly human, they behaved completely like wild beasts. They walked on all fours and snarled and showed their teeth to anyone who came near. They lapped water out of a bowl and howled when they were unhappy.

Adapting to Life in the Wild

Their time in the forest with the wolves had completely changed the girls' bodies. Their jawbones and canine teeth had grown longer. Like wolves, their night vision had become very keen, and they liked to roam the missionary compound at night. They could hear the slightest sound from miles away and could smell raw meat from a distance. When Amala, the youngest, died of an illness, Kamala wandered the house sniffing Amala's clothes, bowl, and bed, searching for her.

Kamala lived with the Singh family for eight more years. She learned to speak a few words but never really adapted to life among humans. When she died at the age of 16, Kamala was still the little wolf child that had been found deep in the forests of India.

* * *

AMAZING KIDS

- Sixteen-year-old Elif Bilgin of Turkey slipped into the finals in Google's 2013 science fair with a project based on…banana peels. Her brilliant idea? To make plastic from them. Elif's banana peel bio-plastic can replace traditional petroleum-based plastics to make everything from cosmetic prostheses (devices to replace missing body parts) to cable insulation.

- Thirteen-year-old Aleix Spiride of Texas got into the Google finals by studying squid. Watching squid jet around underwater gave him the idea for the Squid-Jet. It's a jet-propelled propulsion system that can reach speeds of more than 30 centimers per *second.* Zip-p-p!

BELLY BUTTONS

*Some people have innies and others have outies,
but we all have one. Why? And what
do they do for us? Read on.*

NAVEL EXERCISES

The most common name for the belly
button is *navel*, from an Old English
word that means "the center." The
Romans called the belly button the
umbilicus, after the umbilical cord.
For the Greeks, it was the *omphalos*,
meaning "knob" or "hub." But what is it?

Your belly button is the spot where
your umbilical cord once joined you to your
mother's placenta (that's the organ inside
the mother that brings food and oxygen
to the baby, and draws off waste). Moments after you were born,
the doctor or midwife cut your umbilical cord and tied the end
attached to you into a knot. That became your very first scar.

Most of your body is covered with a layer of fat that plumps up
your skin, but at the belly button the skin attaches directly to your
abdominal wall, like a stitch between two pieces of fabric. That's
why most belly buttons are indented.

NAVEL IDEAS

Once you are born, your belly button has no real function. Some people,
however, refuse to accept that fact and have invented uses for it.

The balata tree, also called the cow tree, has sap that looks and tastes like milk.

Meditation. Have you ever heard the terms "contemplating your navel" or "navel gazing?" Well, there's an official word for it: *omphaloskepsis*—*omphalos* for "navel," and *skepsis* for "the act of looking, or inquiry." An *omphalopsychic* is a person who becomes hypnotized by staring at his own navel.

Christian monks on Mount Athos, Greece, have actually been doing just that since the 10th century. They're called *hesychasts*. Every day they stare at their navels and chant "Lord Jesus Christ have mercy on me, a sinner." They believe that if they do this long enough, they will become one with God.

Telling the Future. Some people read tea leaves to tell the future; others read palms. Then there are those who read belly buttons. *Omphalomancy* is an ancient form of fortune telling in which the number of children a girl will later bear is determined by counting the knots in her umbilical cord at birth.

* * *

DO ANIMALS HAVE BELLY BUTTONS?

Fish, reptiles, birds, and insects don't—their young are nourished inside of eggs, not by umbilical cords. Only mammals have belly buttons...and not even *all* mammals. *Marsupials*, like kangaroos and opossums, have pouches in which their young develop—they don't have umbilical cords, which means they don't have navels. Most mammals, however, including dogs, cats, humans, mice, gorillas, cows, yaks, elephants, and whales, do.

An average honeybee produces one-twelfth of a teaspoon of honey in its life.

ACRONYM QUIZ

An acronym is a word composed of the first letters of each word in a phrase. For example, SWAK stands for Sealed With A Kiss. See if you can match these common acronyms with their correct meanings.

I. ASAP
a) American Students Against Poetry
b) A Seriously Annoying Person
c) All Scars Are Permanent
d) As Soon As Possible

2. AWOL
a) Access While OnLine
b) Absent WithOut Leave
c) Authentically Written Obsolete Language
d) Australian Wallaby Outback League

3. NASA
a) Noble Association of Spacemen and Astronauts
b) North American Strategic Alliance
c) New Approach to Saving America
d) National Aeronautics and Space Administration

4. NATO
a) North Atlantic Treaty Organization
b) Nations Against Total Obliteration
c) Not Another Time Out
d) Nepalese Alliance of Trained Orangutans

Pouring soy sauce on rice is considered offensive in Japan.

5. LASER

a) Liquid Accumulated to Shoot Electric Rays

b) Lethal Atomic System and Elimination Refractor

c) Low Alpha Stream Energy Release

d) Light Amplification by Stimulated Emission of Radiation

6. MASH

a) Mobile Army Surgical Hospital

b) Medical Aid-Station and Housing

c) Military Ambulance Safe Haven

d) Mothers Against Shaggy Haircuts

7. NIMBY

a) Next Idea Might Be Yours

b) Not In My Back Yard

c) Need It Manufactured By Yesterday

d) Now I Mean Business, Y'all

8. RADAR

a) Red Alert Detect And Retaliate

b) RAdical Dish-Activated Recognition

c) Readable Ambitron Device And Recorder

d) RAdio Detection And Ranging

9. SCUBA

a) Self-Contained Underwater Breathing Apparatus

b) Submerged Civilian Utilizing Backpack Air

c) South Carolina University Bathospheric Army

d) Situation Critical: Unstable Breathing Atmosphere

Answers:

1. d; 2. b; 3. d; 4. a; 5. d; 6. a; 7. b; 8. d; 9. a

Internet is an acronym for "International Network."

GET REAL!

What's the biggest new TV fad? Reality shows.
Here are the origins of some favorites.

AMERICAN IDOL

Simon Cowell may seem mean when he puts down contestants on *American Idol*, but he's allowed to be: it's his show. Besides, he really knows his stuff. In the 1990s, Cowell created the British boy bands Five and Westlife, who racked up 10 number-one hits between them.

In 2001 he teamed up with Simon Fuller, creator of the Spice Girls, to create a TV show called *Pop Idol*. Concept: Thousands of contestants would audition for a chance to get on the show, only a few dozen would make it, and viewers would pick the winner.

The show was a huge hit in England, so the two Simons created versions for Canada, Germany, Norway, Poland, the Netherlands, the Middle East, and South Africa. But nowhere has it been more successful than in the United States. *American Idol* became an instant hit for Fox TV. The show has produced a string of singing stars including Kelly Clarkson, Ruben Studdard, Carrie Underwood, Fantasia Barrino, and Clay Aiken.

SURVIVOR

Another show that began in Europe, *Survivor* is actually based on two classic novels: *Robinson Crusoe* and *Swiss Family Robinson*, both about civilized people forced to survive on a deserted island. The show was created by an Englishman named Charlie Parsons. He called it *Expedition Robinson*, and when it premiered on

Scientists say that stupid people laugh more than smart people.

Swedish television it was very popular, airing seven nights a week. From there it spread across Europe and eventually to the United States, where it was renamed *Survivor* and became the most-watched primetime show on CBS.

THE BACHELOR

In 1925 a movie called *Seven Chances* was released. It was about a man who will inherit his grandfather's fortune if he gets married by 7 p.m. on his 27th birthday. He has to pick among dozens of eligible women to get his $1 million but only has a few hours in which to choose. The movie was remade in 1999, this time titled *The Bachelor*, starring Chris O'Donnell. Executives at ABC, who were trying to find their own reality TV hit, decided to create a new show based on the concept.

FEAR FACTOR

Reality show producer J. Rupert Thompson loves action movies (and *Jackass*) so much that he decided to make an action reality show. "It's all about the stunts, and how contestants navigate the crazy environments we put them in," says Thompson. "If we don't make the stunts scary or gross enough, then we don't have a show."

• **Memorable stunts:** Being dragged by a horse, crawling through rancid water, lying down in a snake pit, and getting attacked by dogs.

• **Gross eating dares:** Beetles, worms, sheep eyes, cow eyeball juice, crickets, cow brains, and live snails.

Old folk remedy: To cure bed-wetting, eat a mouse.

RESCUE TURTLE

*Look! Down in the water! It's a fish!
It's a submarine! No, it's Rescue Turtle!*

TURTLE LIFE RAFT

In 1975 a woman was shipwrecked in the waters off the coast of Manila, in the Philippines. Completely alone and far from land, she was certain her life would soon be over.

Suddenly she saw a giant turtle swimming toward her. Desperately, she flung her arms around the turtle's shell, holding on for dear life. The turtle began swimming. For two days the turtle swam with the woman on its back, towing her toward land. Not once did it dive underwater, which sea turtles need to do to find food. For some reason, the turtle was so determined to save the woman that it gave up eating.

A cruise ship finally spotted the woman floating in the sea. The crew thought she was clinging to an empty oil drum, so imagine their surprise when the "drum" began swimming circles around the woman! The remarkable turtle continued to circle until she was rescued, then it dove beneath the waves and disappeared.

FISH FRIGHT

Uncle John's advice: Do not pick up, poke, tease, kick, or step on any blobby, jellylike creature—or anything else—while on the beaches of Australia.

POISON IN PARADISE!

Australia's Great Barrier Reef is home to some of the most dangerous sea life in the world, such as the tiger shark and the barracuda. But it's the smaller creatures—some no larger than a peanut—that make this wildlife refuge *really* scary. Meet six of the most dangerous sea creatures on the reef—and in the world.

I. BOX JELLYFISH

Description: The body of a box jellyfish (also known as a sea wasp) is the size of a human head. Pale blue and transparent, it has about 15 long tentacles on each corner of its box-shaped body. Running the length of each tentacle are thousands of stinging cells. It may look like a lifeless blob, but the box jellyfish can swim at a speed of 5 feet per *second.*

Watch Out! If you get tangled up in its 10 feet (or more) of tentacles, you could die within 30 seconds—unless you get the antidote right away.

2. BLUE-RINGED OCTOPUS

Description: This little octopus never grows larger than a golf ball. When it's relaxed, it is yellowish brown. But when it's angry or frightened, little blue rings appear on its body, and it starts biting. By the time you see the rings, it's probably too late!

Watch Out! The poison can kill a human being. You may not even know you've been bitten until the symptoms kick in: extreme pain, nausea, blurred vision, and paralysis. Now for the bad news: There is no known antidote for a blue-ringed octopus bite.

3. IRUKANDJI JELLYFISH

Description: These peanut-size deepwater jellyfish are transparent. They have a box-shaped bell with a single long tentacle hanging from each corner.

Watch Out! The toxins from these tiny jellies are so powerful that every summer they put an average of 60 people in the hospital. The sting is extremely painful...and sometimes deadly.

4. CONE SHELLS

Description: These colorfully striped or spotted, cone-shaped snails live around mud flats and in shallow reef waters. Their shells are beautiful, but don't pick one up! Inside lurks a sea snail with a single harpoonlike tooth. These poisonous creatures come in all sizes: some are as small as a fingernail, others as big as a football.

Watch Out! The cone shell's tooth is so sharp it can penetrate clothing. And the bite packs a real wallop: weakness, lack of coordination, blurred vision, numbness, pain, and, in severe cases, death.

Looney law: In Berea, Kentucky, dogs and cats must wear taillights after dark.

5. LIONFISH

Description: The colorfully striped lionfish gets its name from the long, sharp, extremely poisonous spines that are spread out along its back like a lion's mane.

Watch Out! You probably won't see any lionfish—they hide motionless in crevices, waiting for dinner to come to them. But if you *do* brush against one, you'll know it right away. The sting site will swell rapidly. You'll become nauseous, have trouble breathing, go into convulsions, and collapse. Most people survive a lionfish sting, but it can take months to get over it.

6. STONEFISH

Description: Lying low in the mud, hiding out on coral reefs, or lurking near rocks, the stonefish is naturally camouflaged with brown and green patches. But this fish also has 13 dorsal spines, each of which squirt venom when pressed against.

Watch Out! Keep your hands out of the rocks and coral! A stonefish sting will cause blinding pain, rapid swelling, muscle weakness, temporary paralysis, and, if left untreated—death.

Is your male fish blowing bubbles? That means he is ready to breed.

G ASTLY HUMO

Uncle John likes a good gag. (These jokes made him sick.)

Q: What goes Ho, ho, ho!— *plop?*
A: Santa Claus, laughing his head off.

Q: What kind of mistakes do ghosts make?
A: Boo-boos.

Q: Why are ghosts bad at telling lies?
A: Because you can see right through them.

Q: What do you call a skeleton who presses a doorbell?
A: A dead ringer.

Q: What's invisible and plays soccer?
A: A ghoulie.

Q: What do cannibals call skateboarders?
A: Meals on wheels.

Q: Why is a ghost like an empty house?
A: Because there's no-body there!

Q: What happened when the ghost disappeared in the fog?
A: He was mist.

Q: What do you get when you cross a Cocker Spaniel, a Poodle, and a ghost?
A: A cocker-poodle-boo!

Q: Why did the cannibal get expelled from school?
A: He was buttering up his teacher.

Q: What plant do you get when you cross a firecracker with a ghost?
A: Bam-boo!

The Bible contains the phrase "Ha, ha." (Job 39:25)

MESSAGE IN A BOTTLE

Imagine you're swimming in the ocean and suddenly a bottle floats by. Inside is a message from someone in a far-off place. It could be a surprise gift, a plea for help...or even a message from beyond the grave.

LUCKY FIND

In 1937 Daisy Singer Alexander, heiress to the Singer sewing machine fortune, made up a will, stuffed it in a bottle, and tossed it into the Thames River in London, England. The will read: "I leave half my estate to the lucky person who finds this bottle."

Twelve years later, in 1949, an unemployed man named Jack Wrum was wandering along a San Francisco beach when he found the bottle. He opened it, read the will, and took it seriously enough to find out if it was real. Amazingly, it was. Wrum inherited $6 million in cash, plus an income of $80,000 a year (for the rest of his life) from Daisy Alexander's Singer stock.

MAN'S BEST FRIEND

Robert Sinclair was a 55-year-old hermit who lived alone in a broken-down farmhouse outside Falkirk, Scotland. Suffering from chronic asthma, he collapsed on the floor one day. Sinclair was too weak to get up but managed to write a note asking for help and put it in a bottle. He pulled himself to the window and threw it outside.

Sinclair went eight days without food and four days without

water. He was near death when Ben, a sheepdog from a nearby farm, found the bottle and took it to his master. Brian Besler read the note inside the bottle:

> I'm in severe pain and cannot move from this house. I've run out of food and I don't want to die here. Please help.
> —Robert Sinclair

Besler called emergency services, who rushed to the old farmhouse. Sinclair was barely alive and struggling for breath when they found him. He was given oxygen and rushed to a hospital, where he made a full recovery. If Ben the sheepdog hadn't found the bottle with the note inside, Sinclair would have died.

MESSAGE FROM BEYOND

When Roger Clay was seven years old, he went to Florida on vacation with his family. One day he wrote a note, put it in a bottle, and tossed it into the Gulf of Mexico.
The note read:

> To whoever finds this letter,
> please write me a letter and let me know.

He signed his name and included his address in Fairfield, Ohio. The note was dated December 27, 1984.

Sadly, Roger Clay was killed in a motorcycle accident when he was 21. But his parents were to receive one last message from him,

four years after he died: In 2003, Don Smith found the bottle floating in the water behind his house in Tampa, Florida. It had been drifting in the Gulf of Mexico for 19 years! When Smith returned the letter to the Clays, Roger's father said, "It's kind of hard to put into words, all the emotions that brings back. It was like Roger was trying to remind us he was still with us."

*   *   *

FLUBBED NEWS HEADLINES

MARCH PLANNED FOR NEXT AUGUST

Astronaut Takes Blame for Gas in Spacecraft

Kids Make Nutritious Snacks

PATIENT AT DEATH'S DOOR— DOCTORS PULL HIM THROUGH

Local High School Dropouts Cut in Half

IRAQI HEAD SEEKS ARMS

FAMOUS PIRATES

Long John Silver? Jack Sparrow? Captain Hook? Those movie pirates don't begin to compare to the real deal.

BLACKBEARD

The Big Daddy of all pirates was Edward Teach, better known as Blackbeard. For five years, until he met his end in 1718, he terrorized the Atlantic Coast from the Bahamas all the way to Maryland. Blackbeard liked to look as terrifying as possible. Standing 6' 5" tall, he was a huge man of great strength. To look even more fierce, he would braid lit bomb fuses into his long black hair and beard before an attack.

The sight of this wild-haired giant standing on his ship, sword in one hand and pistol in the other, with clouds of smoke pouring from his head, laughing like a maniac, convinced sailors that the Devil himself was after them. They usually surrendered their ships without a fight, which was exactly what Blackbeard wanted.

Like most pirates, Blackbeard had only a brief reign as scourge of the seas. During a furious naval battle near his base in Bath, North Carolina, he was finally beaten on November 22, 1718. The victorious British captain cut off Blackbeard's head and tossed his body overboard to the sharks. Legend has it that the headless body swam around the ship three times looking for its head before sinking beneath the waves.

HENRY MORGAN

This is one pirate captain who beat the odds and came out on top. Born in Wales in 1635, Henry Morgan shipped out to the Caribbean to seek his fortune as a privateer—a pirate who is given permission by one country to raid the ships of its enemies.

By 1668 Morgan was the commander of a fleet of pirate vessels working for England against their archrivals, the Dutch and the Spanish. At one point Morgan had 36 ships and 2,000 sailors under his command. He raided ships from Venezuela to Cuba, and was feared by his enemies for his brutality.

In 1671 he invaded Panama, the heart of Spain's American empire, and brought back looted treasure to his base in Jamaica. But unbeknownst to Morgan, Spain and England had declared peace. Suddenly, he was no longer a legal privateer fighting for England but was considered a criminal raiding the ships of England's friend and ally. Result: He was arrested and sent back to England to stand trial.

Fortunately for Morgan, the Spanish and English started fighting again, and he was knighted for his heroic actions on behalf of the crown. He returned to Jamaica as Lieutenant Governor, and retired to his plantation a wealthy man.

CAPTAIN KIDD

It was William Kidd's bad luck to become a pirate at the wrong time. Captain Kidd sailed from London in 1695 as a privateer, with permission from the British government to raid the pirates of the Red Sea. He was to bring the loot home to England, where the investors who paid for his trip (including the king of England) would split the plunder.

By the time Kidd reached the Red Sea, two years had passed

Many world cultures forbid eating with the left hand. It's considered unclean.

and the British government had changed its policy—it now wanted nothing to do with privateers. Why? Because these legalized pirates were too hard to control, brought complaints from other nations, and (most importantly) were no longer a major source of income to the crown.

Unfortunately, Kidd didn't know that change was in the wind, and captured a rich merchant vessel from India. India promptly complained, and British authorities declared Kidd a pirate and a criminal. The British Navy chased Kidd all the way across the Atlantic to New York City, where he was arrested and sent back to England in chains.

The trial lasted all of one day; Kidd was found guilty and hanged. (There's no record of what happened to the loot...or if the king of England got his share.)

* * *

SCIENTIFIC NAMES FOR GROSS STUFF

Runny nose: *Rhinorrhea*

Scab: *Fibrinogen*

Throwing up: *Emesis*

Dandruff: *Pityriasis capitis*

Belch: *Eructation*

Pus: *Purulence*

Ear wax: *Cerumen*

Zits: *Acne vulgaris*

Old-strich? An ostrich can live to be 70.

RECORD
BREAKERS

*The BRI "Golden Plunger" Awards, where Uncle
John recognizes extremes of every kind.*

OLDEST CITY: Damascus, Syria. People have lived there continuously since 6000 B.C. New evidence suggests the town may even date back to 8000 B.C.

COUNTRY THAT EATS THE MOST CHOCOLATE: Switzerland. The Swiss eat about 22 pounds of chocolate per person a year. (The average American eats about half that amount.)

BESTSELLING BOOK OF ALL TIME: The Bible. It's sold more than *6 billion* copies worldwide.

OLDEST TREE: "Methuselah." It's a bristlecone pine in the White Mountains near Big Pine, California. Although you can visit the grove where Methuselah lives, its exact location is a secret. Scientists believe the tree to be 4,767 years old—older than the great pyramids of Egypt.

COUNTRY THAT MAKES THE MOST MOVIES: India. During the 1990s, India produced an average of 851 movies per year—twice as many as Hollywood.

LARGEST LOBSTER: Forty-four pounds, six ounces —about the average weight of a five-year-old child. It was caught near Nova Scotia, Canada, in 1977.

India's movie-making capital, Bombay, is nicknamed "Bollywood."

TREK*NOLOGY

Sci Fi author Arthur C. Clarke once said that "advanced technology is indistinguishable from magic." Uncle John says, "It's also indistinguishable from Star Trek.*"*

TV TECH

When *Star Trek* premiered on TV in 1966, the space technology invented by the show's writers looked like, well, science fiction to viewers. While Captain Kirk and his crew streaked through space at warp speed, "boldly going where no man has gone before," real astronauts could only orbit the Earth a few times before splashing down into the ocean. Even though most people thought it would be hundreds of years before humans developed technology to match Star Trek's, some innovative thinkers were already turning TV fiction into everyday fact. Here are a few examples of how "Trek*nology" has become *tech*nology.

I. SHUTTLE CRAFT

Trek*nology: When Kirk and his crew needed to move people and equipment from the *Enterprise* to a planet's surface, they often used the shuttle craft—a small space vehicle that could go from ship to planet or star base, and back again.

Technology: Fifteen years after the first *Star Trek* episode, NASA launched the first space shuttle. Since 1981 there have been more than 100 shuttle flights. Today, astronauts and supplies are routinely ferried to and from the International Space Station.

2. STAR BASE

Trek∗nology: When the *Enterprise* needed repairs, or the crew needed some R&R ("rest and relaxation"), they set course for the nearest star base—a floating space city that supported hundreds, sometimes thousands, of people with food, housing, and entertainment.

Technology: On May 14, 1973, the United States launched the space station Skylab, the home base in space for U.S. astronauts until February 1974. The Russian space station MIR circled Earth from 1986 to 2001. In 1998 the International Space Station began its service as Earth's "star base."

3. PHASER

Trek∗nology: When exploring an alien planet, the crew of the *Enterprise* had to be ready for anything. Their best defense? The *phaser*—a handheld ray gun. Set on "stun," a phaser would merely immobilize the enemy; set on "maximum," it would vaporize him.

Technology: We don't have phasers yet, but a California company is trying to design one. Their suitcase-sized phaser (they call it an "Anti-Personnel Beam Weapon") uses a laser beam to temporarily immobilize the target. It doesn't cause injury, but within milliseconds of being zapped, the suspect is frozen in the position he was in at the moment of being stunned. When this technology is perfected, it will be reserved for military and police use.

State dance of both Washington and Oregon: square dance.

4. COMMUNICATORS

Trek*nology: These small portable communication devices could be used anywhere, anytime, and also worked for remote tracking and locating. No operators. No phone booth. No dangling cord. *Sweet!*

Technology: The first cellular phone call was made in April 1973, but it wasn't until 1982 that cell phones became available to the public—16 years after the first *Star Trek* episode. Today, cell phones not only act as communications devices, they can also log onto the Internet or offer GPS (Global Positioning System) navigational information. And they are even smaller than the communicators Spock and Kirk used.

5. TRANSPORTER

Trek*nology: "Beam me up, Scotty!" Within seconds, Captain Kirk and his landing party would vanish from a planet's surface and reappear in the transporter room on the *Enterprise*. Teleportation—a means of transporting people from one place to another by converting them into pure energy, then changing them back into people again at the other end—was a staple of every *Star Trek* episode.

Technology: Scientists haven't been able to teleport a person (or even an object) from one place to another, but in 1998 they

did succeed in teleporting a laser beam. When it's perfected, this technology will most likely be used for moving information—called *quantum computing*—and will allow people to move huge blocks of digital data at the speed of light. No more twiddling your thumbs while you download your favorite game or MP3 file. But you'll have to wait a little longer before you can say "Beam me up, Scotty."

*   *   *

WHO DONE IT?

He who smelt it, dealt it.

She who discerned it, burned it.

He who derided it, provided it.

She who nosed it, composed it.

He who detected it, effected it.

She who denied it, supplied it.

He who policed it, released it.

She who smelled it, expelled it.

He who snifted it, gifted it.

She who deduced it, produced it.

He who noted it, floated it.

THE GREAT PEBBLE

*If you had this one in your rock collection,
you wouldn't need any more rocks.*

ROCK STAR

The largest free-standing rock in the world sits in the middle of
the Australian Outback. A surveyor named it Ayers Rock in 1873
after Sir Henry Ayers, who was the premier of South Australia at
the time. But the Aborigines, the native people of Australia, had
named this amazing rock thousands of years before Sir Henry was
born. They called it *Uluru*, which means "great pebble."

Uluru rises 1,100 feet above the desert floor, and is 2 ¼ miles
long and 1 ½ miles wide. But that's just the top of it. Most of the
rock lies underground, extending 3 miles below the surface.

How it came to be in the middle of the Australian desert is still
being debated by geologists. The most widely held theory is that
a great deposit of sedimentary rock was created 600 million years
ago and that then this bed of rock was tilted, probably by violent
earthquakes, until it stuck straight up out of the ground.

LIGHT SHOW

Uluru is covered in a layer of iron oxide, which gives it a reddish
tint. But during the day, the play of sunlight on the rock makes it
seem to change colors. It might glow bright red in the afternoon,
then change to orange and then to deep purple by evening. The

traditional Aboriginal belief is that there is a light source deep inside Uluru that causes the color changes.

In fact, every crag, crack, water stain, crevice, and cave of the rock has a meaning to the Aborigines. They believe this sacred rock was created by Kuniya (a python), Kurpany (an evil, doglike creature), and Mala (a wallaby-like creature) at the very moment of creation, which they call Dreamtime.

PAINTED MEMORIES

The insides of the caves around the base of the rock are covered with paintings made by the Aborigines over centuries. The most recent were done in the 1930s, but some of them are thousands of years old. The Pitjantjatjara and Yankunytjatjara tribes have lived near Uluru for 10,000 years, and have used its cave walls to record a visual history of their peoples. Some of the caves are for women only, some are for men, but all of them are considered holy places.

Uluru remained relatively untouched even after Europeans arrived in Australia because it is in one of the most remote areas of the country. Today, however, it is a popular tourist spot, and that's a problem. Visitors aren't always respectful of the rock or the traditions of its owners. Result: The Australian government has had to restrict access to it. But you can still visit Uluru if you ever go to Australia. It's in Uluru-Kata Tjuta National Park in the Northern Territory.

An underground fire in Australia has burned continuously for 2,000 years.

WORD PLAY

Concealed in each puzzle below is a common
word or phrase. Can you guess what it is?
(Answers are on page 284.)

1.

Head
Heels

2.
CHIMADENA

3.
M CE
M CE
M CE

4.
XQQQME

5.
ARREST
YOU'RE

6.
MEREPEAT

7.
A B C D
E F G H J
M O P Q
R S T U V
W X Y Z

8.
$0 ALL
ALL ALL
ALL

9.
YYYGUY

10.
po**FISH**nd

11.
N
I
A
G
A
R
A

12.
Wear
Polka Dot

13.
History
History
History

Q: What is a *heliologist*? A: Someone who studies the sun.

ST ANGE SPO TS

Do you think that baseball is dull? Or that
soccer is boring? Perhaps you'd be interested
in an exciting match of elephant polo.

ELEPHANT POLO

Out of the choking dust appears a grumbling, rumbling, tumbling
mass of gray pachyderms. Somewhere in the center of this mass
is a three-inch ball. *Whack!* Someone hits the ball. The herd
shifts and the dust is kicked higher. *Thwack!* The ball is hit again.
Loud trumpeting blares across the hill. Then, in the shuffling mix
of elephants, men, sticks, and ball, *Splat!* Someone hits a pile
of elephant dung. "Oops—sorry about that, mate." The game
continues.

Rules of the Game

Regular polo is played using teams of horses; elephant polo is
played with two teams of four elephants. Playing time is two
10-minute *chukkers* with a 15-minute rest period in between. Each
elephant carries a polo player and a *mahout* (pronounced ma-
HOWT), or driver. The mahout sits directly behind the elephant's
ears and directs the beast using his voice, hands, and feet. The
player sits behind the mahout and hangs onto the elephant while
striking at the ball with a long-handled mallet. The umpire watches
the play from a wooden *howdah* (platform seat) on the back of
another elephant.

Not only does the umpire need to stop the game every now
and then to bring out a giant pooper-scooper, but he also has to
make sure the elephants don't cheat...which they love to do.

Elephants are not allowed to pick up the ball with their trunks and just toss it into the goal. Nor are they allowed to lie down in front of the goal. Other than that, the game is very much like regular polo—only louder.

World Championship

The annual World Elephant Polo Championship is held high in the Himalayan kingdom of Nepal. This contest attracts teams from many countries, including Great Britain, the United States, Iceland, and South Africa. The 2003 title was won by the Tiger Tops Tuskers from Iceland.

COCKROACH RACES

Billed as the "greatest gathering of thoroughbred cockroaches in the known universe," the World Championship Cockroach Races are

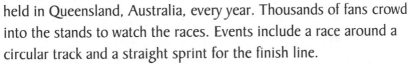

held in Queensland, Australia, every year. Thousands of fans crowd into the stands to watch the races. Events include a race around a circular track and a straight sprint for the finish line.

Cockroach Gold Cup

But the main event is the Story Bridge Hotel Gold Cup. In this race, 20 roaches are placed under a can in the middle of a six-meter (20-foot) ring. The can is raised...and *they're off!* The first roach to escape the ring wins the cup.

OSTRICH RACES

Two thousand years ago, Queen Arsinoe of Egypt rode an ostrich with a saddle. Ancient Romans used teams of these giant birds

to pull carts in chariot races. In the early 1900s, jockeys rode ostriches in races throughout the U.S. and Europe.

Today fans flock to ostrich races in South Africa and many places in the western United States, including Chandler, Arizona, which holds an annual Ostrich Festival.

Jockeys mount the big birds, who race down a straight track, galloping for the finish line. But ostriches really don't like being ridden. They're sensitive and get upset under pressure. And when they get upset, they start spinning around and around. The only thing the jockey can do is hold on tight and wait—because no human is powerful enough to make an ostrich stop spinning once it has started.

The races can look hilarious—with the ostriches spinning in circles—but the jockeys can actually get seriously injured. Why? Ostriches are big: they stand six to nine feet tall and weigh about 400 pounds. They can kill a grown man with just one kick and can run at a speed of up to 60 miles per hour. If you ever want to ride an ostrich, remember this: don't hold onto its neck—that will only make the bird angry and it will start spinning…and spinning…and spinning!

An insect known as the ant lion spends its entire life walking backward.

SECRET PLACES

Do you have a top-secret hideout?
It can't compare to these.

PLACE: Fort Knox

LOCATION: 45 miles south of Louisville, Kentucky

TOP SECRET! Fort Knox is actually the name of the army base next door to one of the most secret places in the world: the U.S. Bullion Depository. The nation's entire gold reserve is kept there in a two-story underground vault, surrounded by a super-secret fortress. The vault's walls are made of granite, concrete, and steel. The door alone weighs 60,000 pounds!

The Depository has its own Treasury Department defense force, but it's also protected by its next-door neighbor, the U.S. Army. For obvious reasons, details of its security system are kept secret from the public. No one person knows the entire combination to the vault door; many people each know little pieces of it. What's inside? About 368,000 gold bars, each weighing 400 ounces (25 pounds). That's 147 million ounces of gold, which, at the current price of about $400 per ounce, would be worth roughly $58.8 billion!

COOL FACT: That's enough money for one large pizza, one half-gallon of ice cream, and two CDs for you and five friends, every day—for more than a million years!

PLACE: Air Force One

LOCATION: Unknown

TOP SECRET! *Air Force One* is the official jet used by the

president of the United States. Its flight plans are secret, and no other aircraft can ever fly in its path. The Secret Service sends advance teams to check the runways and ground personnel before every flight. Food is bought anonymously so that no one knows who it's for—to avoid the risk of the president being poisoned.

There are even secret areas within the plane that only high-level people can access. Those areas house satellite communications systems, coding and decoding devices, antimissile weapons, and other super-secret technology.

COOL FACT: Two jumbo 747s are generally used as the president's planes, but *any* Air Force plane the president boards immediately becomes known as Air Force One.

PLACE: Granite Mountain Records Vault

LOCATION: 20 miles southeast of Salt Lake City

TOP SECRET! Granite Mountain is where the Mormon Church keeps the genealogical records of millions of families. After decades of gathering research, they have more than two billion individual records from 126 different countries—probably including your family's. The records are guarded vigorously, kept in huge vaults dug deep into the mountain. If you wanted to break in, you'd have to dig through 700 feet of solid granite!

COOL FACT: The church claims that the vaults are so secure, they could survive a nuclear attack.

Only about 5% of incandescent lightbulb energy is radiated as visible light.

HOT SHOTS

Our good friend Marley Pratt, at 18 years old, helped his local fire department fight fires while he was fighting his own battle with cancer. Marley and the kids below prove that you don't have to be grown-up to help others.

HOT SHOTS: The Dragon Slayers
THE SPOT: Aniak, Alaska
WHAT THEY'VE GOT: The Dragon Slayers are a rescue squad that was formed in 1994. What makes them different from other squads? Most of the seven Dragon Slayers are teenagers. They are also Yupik and Athabascan Indians. These teens spend about 400 hours a year in rescue training.

They are often beeped out of school to help in an emergency: fighting fires, rescuing people who have fallen through ice, and searching for lost hikers. What else makes them different? Until recently, all of them were girls.

HOT SHOT: Tyrell Lashley
THE SPOT: Washington, D.C.
WHAT HE'S GOT: Tyrell was just 12 years old when he became a Red Cross volunteer. He joined the youth services team at the National Capital Chapter of the Red Cross in 1999. Tyrell soon realized he wanted to help in disaster

operations but was told he was too young to work in this critical area. Determined to overcome the age barrier, Tyrell spent the next three years studying disaster response and researching ways that young volunteers could participate.

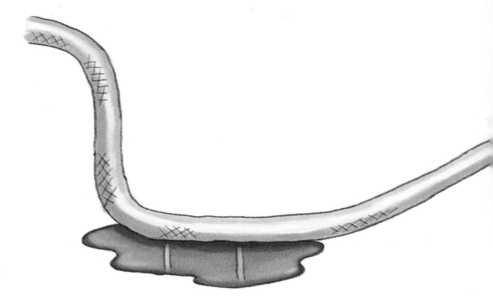

When the September 11 tragedy struck, Tyrell, then 15, volunteered to answer calls at the Red Cross offices and serve as a "home base" while relief teams responded to the crisis at the Pentagon. A month later, during the anthrax crisis, when people feared the deadly poison was being sent through the mail, Tyrell acted as a staffing officer, assisting team members as they went out on emergency calls.

His dedication and training paid off. At 16, Tyrell Lashley became the youngest Red Cross volunteer ever to hold the position of vice chairman of Disaster Services.

HOT SHOTS: Camp Blaze campers

THE SPOT: Pacific Northwest (the location changes every year)

WHAT THEY'VE GOT: At Camp Blaze, girls don't canoe, make arts-and-crafts projects, or sing wacky camp songs. They climb 100-foot ladders, rappel down seven-story buildings, and fight fires in burning cars, dumpsters, and buildings.

Founded in 1999 by eight women firefighters, Camp Blaze gives girls between the ages of 16 and 19 a glimpse of what it's like to be a career firefighter. For an entire week in July, campers get up at 6:30 a.m., do an hour of calisthenics before breakfast, then spend the rest of the day learning the basic skills it takes to be admitted to local fire academies.

Camp Blaze is intended to give girls a head start in a mostly male field, and it's free to all girls with the desire and drive to become firefighters.

It's illegal to leave nude mannequins in New York City store windows.

NAME THAT GOD

The ancient Romans borrowed most of their culture from the ancient Greeks, including their gods. See if you can match the Roman god with its Greek original.

ROMAN

1. Jupiter, king of the gods

2. Juno, queen of the gods

3. Minerva, goddess of wisdom

4. Venus, goddess of love

5. Diana, goddess of the moon

6. Mars, god of war

7. Neptune, god of the sea

8. Aurora, goddess of the dawn

9. Pluto, god of the underworld

10. Cupid, god of love

11. Mercury, messenger of the gods

12. Ceres, goddess of the harvest

13. Vesta, goddess of the home

14. Faunus, god of nature

GREEK

a. Pan

b. Hestia

c. Ares

d. Hermes

e. Zeus

f. Athena

g. Hera

h. Aphrodite

i. Poseidon

j. Eos

k. Artemis

l. Eros

m. Demeter

n. Hades

Answers:

1. e; 2. g; 3. f; 4. h; 5. k; 6. c; 7. i; 8. j; 9. n; 10. l; 11. d; 12. m; 13. b; 14. a

A set of bone false teeth made around 1490 B.C. was found in Switzerland.

DUMB WARS

*Wars are fought for lots of reasons. Land. Honor.
Security. But some wars have been fought
for truly bizarre reasons. Like these.*

WAR OF THE OAKEN BUCKET (1325-1337)

Between: The Italian states of Modena and Bologna

Who Started It: Modenese soldiers invaded Bologna to steal
a bucket. Why? Nobody remembers. They succeeded in getting
the bucket but killed hundreds
of Bolognese in the process.
Bologna declared war to avenge
those deaths…and to get the
bucket back.

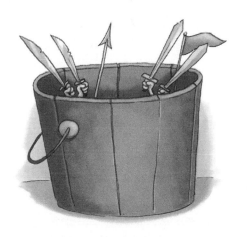

Who Won: The Bolognese
battled the Modenese for 12
years but never did get the
bucket. To this day it's stashed
in the bell tower of a cathedral
in Modena.

WAR OF JENKINS' EAR (1739-1741)

Between: Spain and Great Britain

Who Started It: In 1731 the British merchant ship *Rebecca*, under
the command of Captain Robert Jenkins, was sailing off the coast
of Cuba when it was boarded by a Spanish coast guard sloop (Cuba
was a Spanish colony at the time). The Spanish captain thought
Jenkins insulted him, so he cut off the Englishman's ear. Jenkins kept

the ear and preserved it in a jar. Seven years later, he told the story to the House of Commons and the English public became enraged. On October 23, 1739, the English government declared war on Spain.

Who Won: Nobody. Both sides won a few battles and lost a few battles, but neither ever got the upper hand (or ear). The war ended in 1741...from lack of interest.

SOCCER WAR (1969)

Between: El Salvador and Honduras

Who Started It: The neighboring countries were facing each other in a World Cup soccer match on June 27, 1969. Late in the game, a referee gave El Salvador a penalty kick. They scored from the penalty spot and won, 3–2. When news of the ref's call spread, riots broke out in both capitals. Fans went on a rampage, looting stores and beating up opposition supporters. On July 14, war was declared, and the Salvadoran army launched an attack.

Who Won: The actual war only lasted four days, but 2,000 people were killed and the Central American Common Market—on which both countries depended—collapsed. Result: Serious food shortages. To add insult to injury, El Salvador lost the next round and was eliminated from World Cup competition.

*   *   *

"You can't depend on your eyes when
your imagination is out of focus."

—**Mark Twain**

IT'S ABOMINABLE!

Ever heard of Bigfoot, the big hairy monster said to live in the remote forests of western North America? Well, halfway around the world lives another great hairy beastie.

BIRTH OF A LEGEND

High in the Himalayan Mountains of Asia lurks a legendary race of huge, hairy, humanlike creatures known as Abominable Snowmen. Stories of these strange beasts, covered in thick reddish-brown hair, go back centuries.

The Sherpa people of Nepal call them *yeti*, which means "rock animals." The Bhutanese call them *migyu*, or "wild men." So why do we call them "Abominable Snowmen"? Because of a spelling mistake.

NAME THAT CREATURE

In 1921 British explorer C.K. Howard-Bury led an expedition attempting to climb Mount Everest in Tibet. At about 17,000 feet, where there's nothing but rocky outcroppings and lots of snow, the climbers saw some "shadowy forms" moving across a snowfield. Howard-Bury asked his Tibetan guides what they were. The guides described them as *metoh-kangmi*, which means "snow creature" or "man-sized snow beast."

But when the report reached newspaper columnist Henry Newman of the Calcutta *Statesman*, he botched the term and repeated it as *metch-kangmi*, which translates to "abominable (or disgusting) man of the snow." News of a mysterious wild man in the far-off and desolate Himalayas traveled like wildfire around the world, and the legend of the "Abominable Snowman" was born.

YETI SIGHTINGS

1832: English explorer B.H. Hodson reports being attacked by a "wild man" who "moved erectly, was covered in long, dark hair, and had no tail." The Sherpas call it a *rakshas*, which means "demon."

1889: Another English explorer, L.A. Waddell, finds a trail of giant footprints at 17,000 feet in the Himalayas. His Sherpa guides tell him they're from a yeti.

1951: Mountaineer Eric Shipton takes photographs of giant footprints—13 inches wide and 18 inches long—on Mount Everest. Some experts claim these photos are proof that the yeti really exists.

1958: Dr. Osman Hill of London performs blood tests on a shriveled hand believed to have come from a yeti. The tests reveal the hand is "not human."

1991: The *Unsolved Mysteries* TV show had parts of the hand analyzed at UCLA. Tests confirm that it came from something not human...but "close to human."

YETI "FACTS"

According to legend...

• A full-grown yeti is huge—nearly nine feet tall.

• It has shaggy hair everywhere except on its face.

• Its huge hands can kill a yak (a large, long-haired ox) with a single blow.

• A baby yeti has bright red fur. As it grows older, the fur becomes darker.

- The yeti is nocturnal—it sleeps during the day and hunts at night—and may live as long as 30 years.

- It doesn't actually live in the snow. It lives along the tree line, right below where the snow remains in the mountains all year long. It only goes into the snow to travel from valley to valley.

- Even though there is still no hard proof of its existence, the people of Bhutan, a small country in the Himalayas, have declared the yeti their national animal.

A living red sponge, when pushed through a net, will reassemble itself.

MORE MATH MAGIC

Want to mind-boggle your friends and family?
Follow the instructions below...but don't look at the
answer until you have completed all the steps!

1. Pick a number between 5 and 9.

2. Subtract 5.

3. Multiply by 3.

4. Square the number (multiply it by itself).

5. Add the digits in the number together until you get only one digit. Example: For 64, add 6 + 4 = 10, then add 1 + 0 = 1. For 9, add 9 + 0 = 9.

6. If the number is less than 5, add 5. Otherwise subtract 4.

7. Multiply by 2.

8. Subtract 6.

9. Give the digit its corresponding letter in the alphabet
  (1 = A, 2 = B, 3 = C, 4 = D, 5 = E, etc.).

10. Pick a name of a country (not a state) that begins with that letter.

11. Now take the second letter in the country's name and think of a mammal that begins with that letter.

12. Think of the most common color of that mammal.

Answer:

A Gray Elephant from Denmark. If you didn't get that answer, you either thought of a really unique country and a really unique mammal...or you need to check your math and try again!

Foiled again! Americans use about 8 million miles of aluminum foil each year.

AMAZING COINCIDENCES

The universe works in mysterious ways.
Want proof? Here are six examples.

LATE TRAIN

In 1929 American novelist Thomas Wolfe told a friend that his next book would be about some passengers on a train. He planned to call it K-19, after the number of the railroad car in which the people were riding. He never wrote the story, but when he died in 1938, Wolfe's body was shipped home for burial by train. The number of the railroad car in which his body was placed? K-19!

STRIKE THREE

In 1949 Rolla Primarda of Taranto, Italy, was struck and killed by a bolt of lightning. According to the U.S. Weather Service, the odds of that happening to anyone are about 600,000 to 1. But what makes Primarda's fate so amazing is that his father had been struck down by lightning 20 years earlier in the exact same spot. Even more amazing: 30 years before that, his grandfather had died…in the same place and in the very same way.

SPECIAL DELIVERY

In 1971 Mrs. Willard Lovell of Berkeley, California, accidentally locked herself out of her house. She was struggling to force her way inside when the postman arrived with a letter. Her brother had stayed with her a few weeks before and had forgotten to return the spare key when he left. The key was in the envelope!

OUT OF THE PAST

In the 1920s, American writer Anne Parrish and her husband were browsing in a bookstore in Paris, when she came upon a special children's book. It was a well-worn edition of *Jack Frost and Other Stories*. She immediately showed it to her husband, remarking that the story had been one of her favorites as a little girl. Her husband opened the book and was stunned to read the inscription inside: "Anne Parrish, 209 N. Weber Street, Colorado Springs, Colorado." It was Anne's old book!

DOUBLE WHAMMY

In 1787 Jabez Spicer was killed by two bullets during a skirmish near Springfield, Massachusetts. At the time, Spicer was wearing a coat that had belonged to his brother Daniel—the same coat Daniel had worn when he was shot by two bullets in 1784. Not only that, the bullets that killed Jabez passed through the same holes made by the bullets that had killed his brother three years before!

SECRET AGENT KID

A 15-year-old student at Argoed High School in North Wales, Pennsylvania, went to take his examinations in 1990 and was randomly assigned the examination number 007 by a computer. His name? Bond...James Bond.

In China, if you find a bone in your food, it's customary to spit it out on the table.

STRAIGHT TALK

Sometimes celebs have something worth saying.

"There's plenty of days when I'm like, 'Oh God, why?' But that's just life. Every moment is not perfect."

—**Beyoncé**

"You may go years without winning. That's OK, as long as you keep trying to improve."

—**Tiger Woods**

"My theory is that if you look confident, you can pull off anything—even if you have no clue what you're doing."

—**Jessica Alba**

"I'm not concerned about my weight. I've always been healthy. I eat right. I'm just a big dude. I've always been happy with the person I am."

—**Ruben Studdard**

"Dumb is just not knowing. Ditzy is having the courage to ask!"

—**Jessica Simpson**

"I don't believe that old cliché that good things come to those who wait. They come to those who want something so bad they can't sit still."

—**Ashton Kutcher**

"I think being different, being against the grain of society, is the greatest thing in the world."

—**Elijah Wood**

"Always tell the truth. You might not have many friends, but you'll never have enemies, because people will always know where you're coming from."

—**Pink**

He's no jackass: On a cold, rainy day a horse always stands with its butt to the wind.

THE WIZARD OF OOPS

Even a classic movie like The Wizard of Oz *(1939) can have bloopers. The next time you watch it, see if you can spot these.*

SCENE: At the farm in Kansas, Dorothy slips while walking on a fence and falls into a pigpen.

BLOOPER: When Dorothy gets out of the pigpen, she hasn't got a speck of dirt or mud on her.

SCENE: When Dorothy meets the Scarecrow, he's attached to a pole in a cornfield.

BLOOPER: First his head is above the pole. Then it's below the pole. His position changes several times throughout the scene.

SCENE: Dorothy helps the Scarecrow off the pole.

BLOOPER: Watch the length of her pigtails go up and down nearly six inches throughout the scene.

SCENE: The trees throw apples at Dorothy and the Scarecrow. The Scarecrow backs away and falls down.

BLOOPER: Look carefully at Dorothy's feet. She should be wearing the ruby slippers, but she's not—she's wearing black shoes.

SCENE: At the end of the poppy field scene, Dorothy and her friends link arms while skipping off to the Land of Oz.

Odds that a person will test a new pen by writing their own name: 97%.

BLOOPER: Watch the Cowardly Lion's tail. The "invisible" fishing line holding it up scrapes across the top of some of the poppies, knocking the snow off them.

SCENE: The Lion sings "If I Were King of the Forest."
BLOOPER: His crown falls off his head and bounces...even though it's supposed to be a porcelain flowerpot.

SCENE: When Dorothy and her pals are on their way to get the Wicked Witch's broom, the Cowardly Lion is seen holding an old-fashioned chemical sprayer and a large butterfly net.
BLOOPER: Suddenly, the chemical sprayer and butterfly net disappear and the Lion is holding his tail.

SCENE: Climbing the rocks outside the Wicked Witch's castle, the Tin Man pulls himself up by the Cowardly Lion's tail.
BLOOPER: A block of wood was used to reinforce the tail. It can be seen outlined under the costume.

SCENE: The Tin Man, the Cowardly Lion, and the Scarecrow sneak into the Wicked Witch's castle to free Dorothy. The Tin Man breaks through the door with an ax.
BLOOPER: Where did the ax come from? He wasn't carrying it when he ran up the stairs.

SCENE: Back in the Emerald City, Toto reveals the Wizard standing behind the curtain.
BLOOPER: Toto doesn't use his mouth to pull the curtain aside—

the curtain is tied to the dog's neck. When Dorothy confronts the Wizard, you can see her take the rope off Toto's neck.

* * *

BEHIND THE SCENES IN OZ

• At the beginning of the "We're off to see the Wizard!" scene with the Scarecrow, the Tin Man, and Dorothy, there is a strange movement in the forest behind them. There was a bizarre rumor that it was a member of the crew hanging himself. But it's actually a large bird (possibly a stork) stretching its wings. If you look carefully, you can also find a toucan and a peacock in the Tin Man's forest.

• Margaret Hamilton, who played the Wicked Witch of the West, spent six weeks in the hospital after she was burned while filming the Munchkin scene. Her green face makeup caught fire when she disappeared in a puff of smoke.

• The Cowardly Lion's costume was made of two real lion skins and weighed more than 50 pounds.

• Check out the "horses of a different color" in the Emerald City. The purple one can be seen trying to lick its color off. That's because the horses were painted with colored Jell-O. They liked the taste so much that their scenes had to be filmed quickly before they licked off all their coloring.

In *The Wizard of Oz* book, there are two brick roads—one yellow, the other red.

THRONE AWARDS

Forget the Oscars and the Emmys. These awards really matter.

AWARD: Most Complicated Toilet

WINNER: Ayse Birsel of New York City wins for her toilet, dubbed the Zöe Washlet. Features: a self-lifting lid triggered by a motion detector, a heated seat, and a built-in flush simulator to cover any trumpet noises. It freshens the air after use and even washes and dries your butt for you!

AWARD: Most Expensive Bathroom

WINNER: Everything in Lam Sai-Wing's Hong Kong bathroom is made of 24 carat gold: the toilet, the floor tiles, the mirror frames—even the chandelier. The only thing that's not all-gold is the ceiling, which is studded with 6,200 diamonds, pearls, rubies, sapphires, emeralds and amber. Cost: $3.5 million!

AWARD: Best Top Secret Toilet

WINNER: Marco Schimmel of Holland designed the UriLift urinal. During the day it's hidden under the street beneath what looks like a man-hole cover. At night the UriLift is lifted up to street level by remote control so late night party animals won't use a wall.

THE THRONEY

GUESS I'LL GO EAT WORMS

Entomophagy *is the scientific name for eating bugs. Sound disgusting? Maybe, but people all over the world do it—bugs are packed with protein and nutrients. And, as you already know, the world is crawling with 'em.*

MC BUGS

Satapol Polprapas lives in Thailand and he loves eating insects so much that he created a fast-food restaurant with only bugs on the menu. The restaurant, called Insect Inter, became so successful that Polprapas expanded the operation. Now there are more than 60 locations throughout Thailand. Insect Inter's motto is, "Never mind the look, it tastes great!" Just think, for about 30 baht (70 cents) you can get an order of Cuppa-Critters to go. What else is on the menu? Grasshopper Salad and Cricket Tempura. Yum! Polprapas hopes that "our crispy, crunchy crickets will replace popcorn as the favorite snack in the cinema."

SPECIAL DELIVERY

If you'd like to try insects, but a trip to Thailand is out of the question, why not order your bugs by mail? Insect Inter will ship them to you. For $4 you can get a can of Mixed Insects, which includes mole crickets and water beetles. They're cooked, salted, and ready to eat. Or how about the most popular insect treat in Thailand—giant water bugs. They're great in spicy salads! If that's

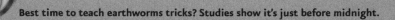

Best time to teach earthworms tricks? Studies show it's just before midnight.

not tasty enough, some connoisseurs also enjoy roasted bamboo worms or fried black scorpions.

BAKING WITH BUGS

Creative chefs use bugs to make candy, fritters, muffins, fried crisps, soup, salad, and even cookies. Here's one of Uncle John's favorite bug recipes, from the Iowa State University entomology department's list of Tasty Insect Recipes.

*   *   *

BANANA WORM BREAD

Ingredients:

½ cup shortening

¾ cup sugar

2 bananas, mashed

2 cups flour

1 tsp. baking soda

1 tsp. salt

½ cup chopped nuts

2 eggs

¼ cup dry-roasted army worms
(a type of yellow-green caterpillar found in fields and gardens)

Directions:

1. Pre-heat oven to 350°F. Rub a little shortening on the inside of a loaf pan.

2. In a large bowl, mix together all ingredients.

3. Pour the batter into the pan, and bake for 1 hour.

4. Remove from oven, let cool, then remove from pan. Cut into ½-inch slices and eat…if you dare.

LION HUNTERS

Why do people do things the way they do? Often it's because that's the way their parents did them. After several generations, the old ways become traditions.

LIONHEARTED WARRIORS

Masai warriors stand out in a crowd. Tall, thin, and muscular, with dark brown skin, these tribesmen from East Africa wear their traditional tunics of bright red cloth that can be seen for miles across the dry plains. Despite centuries of contact with the modern world, these proud warriors continue to live as they always have, according to the customs and ways of their ancestors. They live with their families in villages of dung huts and eat traditional Masai food—mostly a combination of cow's blood and milk.

Of the 42 tribes of Kenya, the Masai are the most famous. Why? Maybe it's because of their reputation as fierce hunters. The Masai own huge herds of cows—and they will do anything to protect their cattle from predators, especially the fiercest predators: lions.

MORANI

When Masai boys turn 15, they are initiated into manhood and become *morani* (warriors). Many years ago, to become a full-fledged *moran*, each boy had to face and kill a lion single-handedly, armed only with a spear. Today, because of conservation laws aimed at protecting lions from being overhunted, the tradition has changed: boys in the same age group *share* a lion kill—but it remains an important part of their coming-of-age ritual.

The Masai language is called *maa*. That's where the name *Masai* comes from.

Other *moran* traditions:

• Once they are accepted as warriors, these young men spend the next five to seven years as a unit. They eat together, drink together, and live together.

• They never go anywhere without their long spears, their swords, and their bows and arrows.

• They wear their hair long and spend hours a day working on their hairstyles, daubing a red-brown mud into the hair and then plaiting it in tight braids. The effect is dramatic—the mark of a Masai warrior.

ON THE JOB

But a *moran*'s main job is to protect his village and its herd of cattle. The Masai don't farm or fish. They roam across the plains with their cattle. In fact, the Masai believe that God gave all of the cattle in the world to them for safekeeping. So they've also become expert cattle thieves, which has caused problems for neighboring tribes and ranchers.

FOOD FOR THOUGHT

The Masai get most of their food from their cattle—milk and blood—which they harvest like milk. They pierce a big vein in a cow's neck with an arrow and catch the blood in a gourd. Then

they mix the blood with milk and let it curdle into custard. This is the Masai daily meal, and it allows them to live off their herds for great lengths of time. Occasionally they eat the meat, but only rarely, and usually as part of a celebration or feast.

THE PASSING OF THE SPEAR

When *morani* reach the ripe old age of 30, they are expected to get married. They shave off their beautiful long braids and become tribal elders. Each elder can marry as many wives as he can afford, but each wife has a family who expects a gift of cattle, and each wife gets her own hut. Once a warrior has settled down and become an elder, he takes on a new responsibility: teaching the next generation of young men the ways of the *morani*.

* * *

IN THE NEWS

In November 2013, Jim Howe arrived promptly at 2:00 p.m. at South Cumberland Elementary School in Crossville, Tennessee, to walk his kids home from school. No such luck. Instead of walking hand-in-hand with his children, the dutiful dad was hand*cuffed* by a sheriff's deputy. Apparently only kids being picked up in cars get to go home at 2:00 p.m. Those who walk can't leave until 2:35. "A rule is a rule," said Deputy Avery Aytes. He gave Howe a choice: wait till 2:35 p.m., or go to jail. Howe waited.

Before he was a film star, Sylvester Stallone worked as a lion cage cleaner.

GAMES RULE!

Here are two more games to teach your friends.

FLASHLIGHT TAG

Number of Players: The more, the merrier

Object of the Game: To tag everyone with the beam from a flashlight

How to Play: This is a great game to play at night in a large backyard or playground. It's just like regular tag, but instead of using your hand to tag someone, you use a beam of light.

One person becomes "It" and gets the flashlight. He counts to 100 while everyone else runs and hides. Armed with the flashlight, It searches for the others. When It spots one of the hiders, he tags the player with the flashlight beam and calls out the player's name. Tagged players must go to jail and stay there until everyone has been tagged. (The first one tagged becomes It in the next game.) Two important rules to remember: 1) Once the game begins, the flashlight must be on all the time, and 2) the "Not-Its" can change their hiding places whenever they please.

MURDER IN THE DARK

Number of Players: Six or more

Object of the Game: To discover the murderer

How To Play: Play this game at night in a dark room. But before you turn out the lights, you need a pencil and several slips of paper—one for each player. On one piece of paper, write "Murderer." On another, write "Detective." Leave the other slips blank. One player shuffles the slips and gives one to each player.

Important: Don't tell anyone else who you are! Now someone counts to three, turns off the lights, and the game begins.

The Murderer stalks the other players in the dark. When he's ready to do the dastardly deed, he taps his chosen Victim on the shoulder. The Victim falls to the ground and makes dying noises (screaming is good). As soon as someone screams, the player closest to the lights turns them on. The Detective then surveys the body and asks each of the remaining players (who have now become Suspects) one question. Suspects can answer truthfully or lie. The Detective names the player she thinks is the Murderer. If the Detective guesses right, she wins; if she guesses wrong, the Murderer wins. (If the Detective is tapped while the lights are out, she says, "Detective is dead. Game over," and the Murderer wins.)

Now collect the slips and start over!

DUMBERER CROOKS

Just when you think they can't get any dumber, they do.

BANK BLOOPER

A man walked into a Bank of America branch in San Francisco and wrote on a deposit slip:

> This is a stickkup.
> Put all you muny
> in this bag.

While he waited to give his note to the teller, he began to worry. What if someone had seen him write the note? They might call the police! He got so scared that he left Bank of America and went to the Wells Fargo bank across the street.

He handed the note to a teller at Wells Fargo who determined from his spelling errors that the robber was not very bright. She told him she couldn't accept his stick-up note because it was written on a Bank of America deposit slip. He would either have to fill out a Wells Fargo deposit slip or go back to Bank of America. Looking defeated, the man said OK and left.

The Wells Fargo teller called the police, who arrested the robber a few minutes later at the Bank of America, where he was waiting in line.

SHOE

*Willie Shoemaker rode horses. He also won races...
lots of them. Some people think he's the best jockey—
maybe even the best athlete—who ever lived.*

SULTAN OF THE SADDLE

In the world of American horse racing, the Kentucky Derby, the Belmont Stakes, and the Preakness are considered the hardest races to win. That's why Willie "Shoe" Shoemaker is considered the greatest jockey of all time—he won the Kentucky Derby four times, the Belmont Stakes five times, and the Preakness twice. But that's not all:

- Six times he rode six winners in a single day.
- Over his career, he won 8,833 races and more than $100 million.
- He was the first jockey to win a $1 million prize.

AND HE'S OFF!

When Willie Lee Shoemaker was born on August 19, 1931, he weighed only two and a half pounds. He was so small that his grandmother used a shoebox as a cradle and set him next to the oven to keep him warm.

Most jockeys are short and light, so the horse won't be slowed down by having to carry any more weight than is absolutely necessary. Shoe's small size led him to horse racing—but it was his iron will that made him a winner. When he was 16, he got his first job working with racehorses at a ranch in California. The boss

The sea horse is the only fish that can grab things with its tail.

fired him because he thought Shoe didn't have the talent to become a top rider, but Shoe wasn't discouraged. He kept riding.

The next year he won his first race, and once he started winning, he never stopped. At 18, he tied for the national championship. In 1951, the year he turned 20, he was horse racing's biggest money winner. At 21, he set a record for most races won in a year (485)—a record which remained unbroken for 20 years.

SOFT HANDS

In the pint-size world of jockeys, Shoe was a half-pint. He was only 4 feet, 11 inches tall, yet there wasn't a rider he faced that he didn't beat at one time or another over his 42-year career. What made him so good?

According to his fellow jockeys, Shoe had "soft hands"—a riding term for a jockey with a sure but gentle feel for the reins. "Willie takes such light hold of a horse," said Hall of Fame jockey Eddie Arcaro, "that he could probably ride with silk threads for reins."

Shoe had his own idea. "The big thing is to relax. Most jocks don't do that. They're tense. I think my relaxation gets across to the horse and makes him want to run. If I were asked to give advice to young riders, the first thing I'd tell them is 'Never get in a hurry.'"

THE AGONY...

Even a winner has bad days and makes mistakes. In 1957 Shoemaker made one of the most famous blunders in horse

The prize money in a horse race is called the "purse."

racing history. He was riding a horse named Gallant Man. They were winning, coming down the home stretch with a comfortable lead. Then, just before the finish line, Shoe stood up in the stirrups, thinking he'd won the race. But he hadn't—he'd misjudged the finish line. Less than a second later, another horse swept past him to the real finish line. After a screwup like that, everyone thought Shoe was washed up.

...AND THE THRILL OF VICTORY

But he wasn't. Willie Shoemaker kept on racing...and kept on winning.

In 1986 he was 54 years old and near the end of his career. That season he rode a horse at the Kentucky Derby, a long shot named Ferdinand. The starting bell rang. The horses took off, Ferdinand running in last place. But Shoe didn't panic—he calmly worked the horse through the crowd until he got close to the leaders. Then he saw a hole open up between the horses and let Ferdinand run. The big horse surged ahead to win the race by two and a half horse lengths.

AN INSPIRATION TO THE END

In 1990, at the age of 58, Shoe finally retired. The following year a terrible car crash left him paralyzed from the neck down. Did he give up? Never. Although confined to a wheelchair, he went back to the track and continued to train the horses he loved. He passed away quietly in his sleep in 2003.

In a *Superman* comic book, boxer Muhammad Ali knocked out Superman...

BODY OF WATER

We take our vitamins. We eat our veggies. But are we ignoring the most important health food of all?

WATER, WATER EVERYWHERE

You are about 66% water. It's in every part of your body. In fact, water makes up:

- 83% of your blood
- 75% of your brain
- 73% of your muscle tissue
- 25% of your body fat
- 22% of your bones
- 2% of the enamel on your teeth

In other words, water is essential—you just can't live without it. People can survive up to a month without food, but no one will make it more than five to seven days without water. Here's what water does for you:

- Carries food and oxygen throughout your body.
- Moves body waste away from your cells.
- Cushions joints.
- Protects body organs and tissues.

DRINK UP!

On average, your body uses as much as 10 cups of water each day through perspiration (sweating), respiration (breathing), and elimination (peeing and pooping). That means you need to drink the equivalent amount of water every day, just to keep up. You need even more if it's extremely hot or cold outside, because your body uses water to regulate your temperature.

If you're playing a pickup game of basketball, climbing trees, or just running around the yard, keep a water bottle handy because strenuous exercise or work makes you sweat even more. The same thing goes for when you're sick.

WATER TIPS

Your water can come in the form of juice, other beverages, and soup—almost anything that's mostly liquid. Here are ways to make sure you get enough fluids on a daily basis:

• Don't wait until you're thirsty to drink because thirst is a sign that you're already dehydrated.

• Add a glass of water or juice to each meal.

• Take a water bottle to school. Drink the whole thing before lunch, refill it, and drink it all again before you go home.

• Bring water with you wherever you go—the movies, soccer practice, or hanging out with your friends.

• Drink water *instead* of soda.

• Be prepared! Drinking more water will make you healthier...but it will also make you have to go to the bathroom more often!

All the water on Earth would fit into a 700-mile cube.

THE JOLLY ROGER

*What's so "jolly" about a black flag with a skull
and crossbones on it? And who's "Roger"?*

THE ORIGIN OF THE PIRATE FLAG

• One story says that the flag (commonly known as the "Jolly Roger") started out as a signal that a plague-infected ship flew to warn other ships to keep away. This black warning flag often had a white cross on it, which in time turned into a skull-and-bones. Pirates first used it to keep other ships from bothering them. Later it became their battle flag.

• Another version of this flag had an hourglass on it, to warn ships under attack that their time to surrender was limited.

• Some pirates ran up a red flag when they wanted another ship to surrender. The red flag meant, "Give up now and you'll live. If you resist, we'll kill you all." This red flag was called *joli rouge*, which means "pretty red" in French. Some historians say the term joli rouge evolved into *Jolly Roger* and the flag eventually became black.

• Others believe the name *Jolly Roger* came from notorious pirates in the Indian Ocean. The common term for an Asian pirate was Ali Raja, meaning "king of the sea." Imagine a pirate with several pints of rum in his belly yelling, "Ali Raja!" That might well have sounded like "Jolly Roger."

WORD WIZARD

Harry Potter's creator—J.K. Rowling—speaks for herself.

"People have said the humor [in the Harry Potter books] is very adult, but I think they underestimate children. It annoys me that people think you have to dumb down for children."

"Read as much as you can. It will give you an understanding of what makes good writing and it will enlarge your vocabulary. And it's fun!"

"There is a lot of comedy in magic, and magic going wrong."

"I've never managed to keep a journal longer than two weeks. I get bored with my life. I prefer inventing things."

"Always have a vivid imagination, for you never know when you might need it."

"The purest joy was when I knew my book was going to be a book—a real book you could see on the shelf of a bookshop."

"It is our choices that show what we truly are, far more than our abilities."

"I think it's important for children to know that adults, too, have problems."

"Wherever I am, if I've got a book with me I have a place I can go and be happy."

"It is impossible to live without failing at something, unless you live so cautiously that you might as well not have lived at all."

"Harry gave me a job to do that I loved more than anything else."

VOLCANO!

*What's the difference between an egg and the Earth? An
egg is a blob of goo covered by a thin shell. And the
Earth is a blob of HOT goo covered by a thin shell.*

HOT ENOUGH FOR YOU?

The hot goo below the Earth's surface is called *magma*—layers and
layers of molten rock and hot gases extending 3,600 miles down,
oozing and stewing in raging heat. Some of the magma is liquid,
but pressure keeps most of it slightly more solid, like tar. And all
of it is amazingly hot.

Thirty miles down, the magma is about 2,000°F. Where the
magma meets the air and oceans, it cools and hardens into the
Earth's rocky crust. That's where we live. It's 3 to 50 miles thick,
and strong enough to support oceans, mountains, and skyscrapers.
And, most of the time, the crust's rocky thickness protects us from
all that powerful heat down there. Most of the time.

RISING UP

Sometimes, however, there's a hole in the crust that lets melted
rock and hot gases escape. What do we call that hole? A volcano,
of course. No one knows the exact number of volcanoes in the
world. Most are under the oceans. About 550 volcanoes on land
have erupted during human history, and there are always about 15
to 20 volcanoes erupting somewhere in the world at any given time.

When magma comes out of a volcano, it's called lava. It's
usually red hot, still about 2,000° F. (more than four times
hotter than the highest temperature of the average kitchen oven).

Ostrich eggshells ae so hard a 250-pound man can stand on one and not break it.

Sometimes it flows out slowly; other times hot gases blow lava, rocks, and cinders out in an explosive eruption.

THE ERUPTION OF PARICUTÍN

In all of human history, there may be only one volcano that humans have seen starting brand new out of the ground. It was near Paricutín (par-ee-koo-TEEN), a farming village in Mexico, in 1943.

Twelve-year-old Simón Jimenez saw it happen. He said it was a very still day when suddenly the quiet was shattered by a big earthquake and weird clunking, bubbling noises from under the ground. He later described it as sounding like a giant trying to clear his throat. Cracks zigzagged across the fields, and it felt to Simón like the rocks beneath him were breaking apart and sliding into a bottomless pit.

He saw a monstrous cloud of black smoke in the distance. Houses must be burning, he thought. Then, when the hot, black cinders started falling from the sky, everybody began to run and the news quickly spread through the town: Houses weren't burning—the smoke and cinders were roaring up from a hole in the cornfields. The village of Paricutín had turned into a volcano!

The eruption lasted for an amazing nine years! By the time it was finished, the entire village was destroyed and where the cornfield used to, be there was mountain—a volcanic cone 1,300 feet high.

LORD OF... THE HOBBITS

J.R.R. Tolkien (1892–1973) wrote some of the best-loved books of all time: The Hobbit *and* The Lord of the Rings. *But where on Earth did he get the idea for Middle-earth?*

THE STORY BEGINS

One hot summer afternoon in the 1930s, a middle-aged professor sat at his desk at Oxford University in England. John Ronald Reuel Tolkien was grading a stack of student exams when he came upon a blank page. Without thinking, Tolkien wrote down the first words that came to mind: "In a hole in the ground there lived a hobbit." He didn't know what a hobbit was. "Names always generate a story in my mind," he said later. "I thought I'd better find out what hobbits were like."

SHIRE INSPIRATION

Although he wasn't aware of it at the time, J.R.R. Tolkien had actually begun to define the imaginary world of hobbits many years before. Born in South Africa, he'd moved to England with his family when he was four. For a time they lived in the West Midlands, a beautiful place of gentle rolling hills, small farms, and quiet country life. It was this setting that he re-created as the land of the hobbits in his famous books.

Icelanders read more books per person than any other people in the world.

ELVISHLY SPEAKING

At an early age, Tolkien had displayed a remarkable gift for languages. As a teenager, he spoke a made-up language called Animalic, which substitutes animal names for words. In Animalic, for instance, the phrase, "Dog nightingale woodpecker forty" means "You are an ass." By the time Tolkien entered Oxford University, he'd already mastered Latin and Greek, so he turned his attention to Norse and Germanic languages...and discovered a wonderland of ancient poems and stories.

It was an old poem from Finland—the *Kalevala*—that had the most influence on Tolkien. He was so captivated by the ancient Finnish language that it became the inspiration for the Elvish language he invented for the elves in his books.

OBJECT OF SACRED POWER

But the magic of the *Kalevala* didn't stop with its words—the story inspired Tolkien, too. The poem tells of a hero who seeks an object of sacred power. While on his quest, the hero comes to understand power and how it changes people. The *Kalevala* is also full of mythical creatures, magical plants, and shape-shifting animals—all elements Tolkien would use years later.

Two lines from the ninth-century poet Cynewulf also had a great influence on Tolkien:

> *Hail, Earendel, brightest of angels,*
> *Over Middle-earth sent to men.*

Middle-earth (or *Middangeard*) was the Old English word to describe the world where humans live—the land between Heaven above and Hell below.

TELLING THE STORY

With Middle-earth and its languages still simmering on the back burner of his mind, Tolkien began to develop his gift for storytelling by making up bedtime stories for his children. Every year, he wrote them wonderful illustrated letters from Father Christmas describing all the news and adventures from the North Pole. His stories were so popular that Tolkien's children often retold them to their friends, who were always eager to listen.

THE LAND OF SNERGS

While he tried out various versions of the hobbit story on his children, Tolkien found inspiration in another children's story, written by E. A. Wyke-Smith. *The Marvelous Land of Snergs* tells the adventures of a "Snerg" named Gorbo and two children, Joe and Sylvia. Snergs are small—maybe three feet tall—but very strong. They love to celebrate and they love to eat. They are always looking for a reason for a feast—even celebrating the day when it is no one's birthday.

Years later Tolkien recalled how much he and his children loved *The Marvelous Land of Snergs* and that it was "probably an unconscious source-book for the hobbits."

HOBBIT HOLES

In 1929 Tolkien helped excavate an ancient Roman temple known as Dwarf's Hill. Beneath the temple, archaeologists found a labyrinth of tunnels from when the Romans occupied England. After the Romans left, the site was abandoned for 1,000 years. People stayed away, scared by stories that the maze of tunnels

Pierce Brosnan owns the typewriter Ian Fleming used to write the James Bond novels.

and crumbling ruins were home to little people, dwarfs, and hobgoblins. Tolkien was charmed by the superstitious rumors surrounding the ruins. Friends of the author later said that visions of little people popping in and out of the holes of Dwarf's Hill inspired Hobbiton.

MR. HOBBIT

Tolkien based hobbit characteristics on…himself. He liked "gardens, trees, and unmechanized farmlands." He smoked a pipe and preferred simple food, and lots of it. He was fond of wild mushrooms and had a simple sense of humor. Whenever possible, he went to bed late and woke up late. He liked to wear fancy waistcoats and he really did not care to travel much. And the gentle professor was more inclined to rescue spiders from the bathtub than to venture forth on a hero's quest.

AFTERTHOUGHT

Tolkien finished *The Hobbit* in 1936, but never expected it to be published—it was only a story he wrote to entertain his children and friends. So no one was more surprised than the shy Oxford professor when it became one of the best-loved fantasy novels of our time.

Sailors, Paper Kites, and Great Egg Flies are all…types of butterflies.

INVISIBLE INK

Behold! Not one, but two recipes for invisible ink. Because you never know when you'll need to write a secret message.

INK RECIPE #1

Ingredients:
Lemon juice
Small bowl (plastic or glass)
Toothpick (or chopstick)
Piece of paper
Candle

I. Pour a little lemon juice into the bowl. Dip the toothpick or chopstick into the lemon juice and then "write" on the paper.

2. Allow your secret message to air dry (don't use heat to dry it) and the message will disappear.

3. To make the message reappear, hold the paper over a burning candle. *Caution:* Hold it far enough away from the flame so you don't set the paper on fire, but close enough for it to get warm.

Note: Don't have any lemons? You can substitute onion juice, milk, or white vinegar.

Prisoners of war have used their own sweat or saliva as invisible ink.

INK RECIPE #2
Ingredients:

½ cup water

2 small bowls (plastic or glass)

1 teaspoon cornstarch

Piece of paper

Toothpick (or chopstick)

10 drops iodine

Sponge

1. Pour half of the water into one bowl and stir the cornstarch into it. Microwave the mixture for 30 seconds, stir, then microwave for another 30 seconds. Let it cool.

2. Dip the toothpick or chopstick into this "ink" to write your message.

3. Let the paper air dry without heat. Your message will become invisible.

4. To make the message visible, mix the iodine with the remaining water in the second bowl. Lightly sponge the piece of paper with the iodine solution. The paper will turn light blue, and the secret message will appear dark blue.

In 2002 scientists heated the University of Georgia for 21 days...

MEET ME IN ST. LOUIS

What do ice cream cones, hot dogs, cotton candy, and peanut butter have in common? These food favorites all got their start at the St.Louis World's Fair of 1904.

ICE CREAM CONE

Charles Menches sold his ice cream in cups, just like every other ice cream seller at the 1904 St. Louis World's Fair. But the weather was hot, and he had so many customers that he ran out of cups! In a panic he looked to see if a nearby vendor might have some spare containers, but all he could find was a guy from Syria selling waffles. Menches quickly bought some and began selling them wrapped around a scoop of ice cream. The substitute became even more popular than the original.

HOT DOG

By the 1890s, Americans were eating thin, long sausages called frankfurters, usually served on a plate with sauerkraut and mustard. Then, at the St. Louis World's Fair, a German vendor named Anton Feuchtwanger introduced the bun. Like the ice cream cone, it was an invention born out of desperation.

Hot dog sellers usually handed out gloves to customers to wear while eating their frankfurters. But at the fair, too many people walked away still wearing them, and Feuchtwanger soon ran out

...by burning leftover food grease.

of spare gloves. He convinced a nearby baker to make frank-shaped rolls as a substitute for gloves. The rolls actually worked better, and the hot dog, as we know it today, was created. (The name hot dog was thought up two years later by a sports cartoonist named Tad Dorgan…but that's another story.)

COTTON CANDY

Variations of this sweet treat have been around for centuries. In the mid-1800s, master confectioners from Europe and the United States spent hours crafting candy Easter decorations out of melted sugar. They used forks and other tined instruments to separate and spin the strands of sugar into delicate threads.

Four different people—Thomas Patton, Josef Delarose Lascaux, John C. Wharton, and William Morrison—claim to be the inventors of cotton candy. By experimenting with a spinning bowl dotted with numerous holes for the heated sugar to emerge as threads, each had found a quick and easy way to make spun sugar. But it was Wharton and Morrison who took their patented cotton candy machine to the St. Louis World's Fair. Not surprisingly, they sold clouds of the sugary confection and it became a big hit.

PEANUT BUTTER

In 1890 Dr. John Kellogg created peanut butter as a healthy protein substitute for his patients with no teeth. Nobody paid much

When cotton candy was first introduced, it was known as "Fairy Floss."

attention to the new product until a man named C.H. Sumner brought peanut butter to—you guessed it—the St. Louis World's Fair in 1904.

As for Dr. Kellogg, he went on to create the best-known breakfast cereal in the world: corn flakes.

*　　*　　*

OTHER FASCINATING THINGS AT THE 1904 FAIR

- Demonstration of the "newfangled" telephone
- Ice-skating rink with a daily "snowstorm" (an amazing feat in the summer)
- Moving picture theater, where most fairgoers saw movies for the first time
- Statue of Theodore Roosevelt sculpted in butter
- Sculpture of a bear made entirely of prunes
- French's Mustard
- Iced tea
- A "health drink" known as Dr. Pepper
- Puffed rice
- A 250-foot-high amusement ride created by a bridge builder from Pittsburgh named George W. Ferris, which he called... the Ferris wheel

HOOP STATS

Highlights from the National Basketball Association.

HIGHEST INDIVIDUAL SCORE IN A GAME: On March 2, 1962, Wilt "the Stilt" Chamberlain scored 100 points for the Philadelphia Warriors against the New York Knicks.

MOST THREE-POINT SHOTS IN A GAME: Kobe Bryant of the Los Angeles Lakers sank 12 three-pointers (9 of them in a row) against the Seattle Sonics on January 7, 2003.

MOST REBOUNDS IN A GAME: Wilt "the Stilt" again. The 7' 1" center pulled down 55 rebounds on November 24, 1960, against the Boston Celtics.

HIGHEST TOTAL SCORE: On December 13, 1983, the Detroit Pistons beat the Denver Nuggets 186–184, for a combined score of 370.

LOWEST TOTAL SCORE: On November 22, 1950, the Ft. Wayne Pistons beat the Minneapolis Lakers by one point, 19–18.

TALLEST PLAYER: Tie! Gheorghe Muresan from Romania and Manute Bol from the Sudan are both 7' 7" tall!

SHORTEST PLAYER: Tyrone "Muggsy" Bogues, 5' 3", played for four NBA teams from 1987 to 2001.

YOUNGEST PLAYER: Andrew Bynum was 18 years, 6 days old when he played his first game for the Los Angeles Lakers on November 2, 2005.

NBA star Dikembe Mutombo's full name: Dikembe...

THE GHOST OF NUMBER 17

"Deliver us from ghoulies and ghosties and long-leggety beasties, and things that go bump in the night!"—Old Scottish saying

MYSTERY MAN

One hundred years ago, a very odd man moved into house Number 17 on a quiet street near the Royal Botanic Garden in Edinburgh, Scotland. The man was handsome and well-built, but strangely shy. He rarely left his 10-room townhouse, and no one ever came to call. His only visitor was an old woman who cleaned the house and brought him groceries. Years passed, and he didn't make friends with a single person in the neighborhood.

Then one day the mystery man suddenly died. Strange men appeared at the house and took his body away. Neighbors wondered: Who were those men? Where did they come from? And where did they take the body? No one ever found out. The cleaning lady locked the windows and doors of the house, never to return. Number 17 sat empty and abandoned for years.

WHO'S TALKING?

Then word began to spread that the house at Number 17 was haunted. Neighbors at Number 16 and Number 18 claimed to hear voices through the walls, usually after midnight. Then, as quickly as they had started, the noises stopped, and people forgot about Number 17…for a while.

...Mutombo Mpolondo Mukamba Jean Jacque Wamutombo.

In 1914, shortly after the start of World War I, the house was bought by an Englishman who decided to turn it into a boardinghouse. The new business was going fine…until the noises returned.

One day while she was cleaning, a maid suddenly heard voices coming from the attic bedroom. She slowly climbed the wooden stairs toward the strange sounds, which grew louder with each step. But when she opened the door, the voices stopped—and the room was empty. Then another maid heard voices coming from the same room. She hurried up the stairs to look, but when she peered inside, she found no one. Still, she had the distinct feeling that someone—or something—was standing beside her.

MARY BREWSTER

That winter the room was rented to a young married couple. The very first night they heard voices all around them and ran screaming into the hall. While the housekeeper tried to calm the terrified couple, a maid named Mary Brewster went into the room to check it out.

Seconds later the housekeeper and the frightened couple heard a shriek of terror. Running into the room, they found Brewster gripping the bedrail, staring wide-eyed at the ceiling. She never told anyone what she saw—in fact, she never spoke another word in her life. She had completely lost her mind.

ANDREW MUIR

Soon everyone was talking about the ghost in Number 17. Some people believed the story, some didn't. One man who did—a

university student named Andrew Muir—offered to help the owner of the house prove the existence of the ghost once and for all.

Their plan was simple: Andrew Muir would go into the room at 10 p.m. and wait until dawn. If he heard anything strange, he would call the owner, who was in the room directly below, by ringing a loud bell.

Less than 10 minutes after Muir went into the room, the bell rang. The owner raced upstairs and burst into the room. There he found Muir, slumped in a chair, his face frozen in an expression of horror. The young student had been frightened to death.

To this day no one knows what Andrew Muir or Mary Brewster saw. The owner sold Number 17 and moved away. The house was boarded up—no one ever lived there again. Years later all of the houses on the street were torn down, ending any chance of solving the mystery of the murderous Ghost of Number 17.

* * *

OH, HORRORS!

Wes Craven, writer/director of creepfests such as *Nightmare on Elm Street* says his favorite word is *plangent*. Never heard of it? Neither had we. But thanks to Craven we now know a plangent is "a loud, reverberating, melancholy sound."

STUNT MASTERS

People often create publicity stunts to draw attention to a new product. One of the best ways is to put the right animal in the wrong place.

HORSES AT THE MOVIES

When a new movie is ready to go to theaters, filmmakers often have a special screening for an invited list of celebrities. Famous people attract TV and newspaper reporters like bees to honey— exactly what the publicist wants. But publicist Marty Weiser broke all the rules when he hosted a premiere for the 1974 comic western *Blazing Saddles*. Instead of famous stars, he invited horses!

Weiser ran a small ad in the *L.A. Times* "calling all horses" to the special screening at a local drive-in movie theater that Weiser had rented. Of course, Weiser made sure there was a snack bar (called the "horsepitality bar") which offered an assortment of "horse d'oeuvres"—a favorite being dried oats served in a popcorn bucket.

On the night of the screening, Weiser waited anxiously in the empty drive-in, not knowing if anyone was coming. Then a police motorcycle entered the drive-in leading a parade of more than 250 horses and riders. Each horse and rider "parked" next to a speaker box and watched the first showing of *Blazing Saddles*.

WHEN PIGS FLY

One day in 1976, the rock band Pink Floyd arranged for a photo shoot for the cover of their album *Animals* in an industrial section of London. Things went just fine until the 40-foot inflatable pig, which the band had custom-built for the shoot, suddenly broke free of its moorings. Caught in the rising heat from surrounding chimney stacks, the pig shot up to an altitude of nearly 18,000 feet. To make matters worse, the sharp-shooter who had been hired to shoot the pig down in the event of an emergency happened to be out to lunch when the pig "escaped."

To everyone's horror, the huge pig floated away, heading toward Heathrow Airport. The pig eventually crashed in a farmer's field, but while it was airborne, pilots in the area were amused to hear air traffic controllers warning, "Pig on the loose! Pig on the loose!" Inflatable pigs soon became a staple at Pink Floyd concerts.

You weigh less when the moon is directly overhead. Why? Its gravitational pull.

LIONS IN A BOX

Selling cars is no easy job, so car makers are always looking for great publicity stunts to get people down to the showroom to look at their newest models. Late one night in the summer of 2003, publicity people at Land Rover—known for making some of the best off-road vehicles in the world—dropped off a mysterious crate labeled WILD ANIMALS in the center of Darmstadt, Germany. The town awoke the next morning to the roar of a lion coming from the crate. People were terrified. Animal lovers were enraged. Who would be so cruel as to cage a poor lion in the middle of the city? And what if the crate broke and the lion escaped?

Police surrounded the crate and approached with weapons drawn. But when they looked inside, they saw no lion. Instead, they saw a TV running a promotional video for Land Rover vehicles punctuated with shots of roaring lions.

POCKET PET

Some say a sugar glider is the ultimate "pocket pet."
A tame sugar glider will sit on your shoulder, ride in your
hair, or nap in your shirt pocket. So what is it?

PETS FROM DOWN UNDER

Sugar gliders are tiny gliding marsupials (which means they have pouches, like opossums and kangaroos) from Indonesia and Australia. They arc about the size of a hamster—five to seven inches long. They're silvery gray with a black stripe that starts just above their nose and goes all the way back to their bushy tail, and they have soft white bellies.

They're called "gliders" because they actually have membranes between their front and hind legs that allow them to glide through the air as much as 150 feet from tree to tree without ever touching the ground—just like a flying squirrel. They eat fruits, veggies, and insects, and love honey. But they got the name "sugar" glider because in the wild they also eat sweet tree sap.

PAL FOR LIFE

Do they make good pets? Yes and no. Sugar gliders are very affectionate. Once one bonds with you, it will always glide back to you, because you become its "nest." But a sugar glider needs lots of attention. You must spend at least two hours a day playing

First known bank: Babylon's Egibi family ran a money-lending firm in 630 B.C.

with it. Why? If you don't play with them, they'll get lonely and depressed and could actually die. And a sugar glider can live to be 15 years old, so you're making a big commitment when you make a sugar glider your pet.

More downsides to these exotic pets: they're nocturnal (more active at night); they're hard to house train (they poop and pee whenever they feel like it); and they have very sharp claws (ouch!).

*   *   *

WHEN GOOD TEACHERS GO BAD

Q: Why was the math teacher arrested?
A: His story didn't add up.

Q: Why was the music teacher arrested?
A: She got into treble.

Q: What happened when the English
teacher was arrested?
A: She got a long sentence!

PAGE OF SEVENS

On page 77 we told you all about the number 7.
Here are some interesting lists of sevens.

Seven Notes in the Musical Scale

1. Do
2. Re
3. Mi
4. Fa
5. So
6. La
7. Ti

Seven Directions
(Polynesia)

1. North
2. South
3. East
4. West
5. Here
6. Up
7. Down

Seven Virtues
(Samurai)

1. *Gi*
(the right decision)
2. *Yu* (valor)
3. *Jin* (benevolence)
4. *Rei* (respect)
5. *Makoto* (honesty)
6. *Meiyo* (honor)
7. *Chugi* (loyalty)

Seven Colors in the Rainbow

1. Red
2. Orange
3. Yellow
4. Green
5. Blue
6. Indigo
7. Violet

Seven Metals Found in Nature

1. Gold
2. Silver
3. Iron
4. Lead
5. Mercury
6. Copper
7. Tin

Seven Deadly Sins
(Christianity)

1. Pride
2. Envy
3. Gluttony
4. Lust
5. Anger
6. Greed
7. Sloth

The Seven Dwarfs

1. Doc
2. Happy
3. Bashful
4. Sneezy
5. Sleepy
6. Grumpy
7. Dopey

Seven Seas

1. Arctic
2. Antarctic
3. North Pacific
4. South Pacific
5. North Atlantic
6. South Atlantic
7. Indian

Seven Castaways
(*Gilligan's Island*)

1. Gilligan
2. The Skipper
3. The Millionaire
(*Thurston Howell III*)
4. His Wife
(*Lovey Howell*)
5. The Movie Star
(*Ginger*)
6. The Professor
7. Mary Ann

THE MONEY PIT

Nobody knows who dug the mysterious pit on Oak Island or why, but one thing's for sure: there's something down there.

TREASURE ISLAND

In 1795 a Canadian teenager named Daniel McGinnis was exploring tiny Oak Island in Nova Scotia when he found a mysterious hole. Beside the hole was an old tree with some of its branches sawed off. The remnants of a ship's tackle (ropes and pulleys used to hoist cargo) were found on one of the remaining limbs. It looked like they had been used to lower something heavy into the hole.

McGinnis was sure he had found a pirate's buried treasure. He went and got two buddies to help him dig. They hit a flagstone only 2 feet down, then barriers of logs at 10, 20, and 30 feet. But no treasure. McGinnis and his friends gave up...but word of their discovery soon spread and treasure hunters from all over the world flocked to the site.

A STRANGE STONE

Simeon Lynds joined in the search in 1803. At 90 feet, his diggers found a large stone with strange symbols carved on it. A few feet later, they struck what one digger said "felt like a wooden chest." But it was too dark to see, so they stopped for the night.

When they came back the next morning, the hole was completely flooded with water. And it somehow kept refilling, even as the workers tried to bail it out. Unable to get to whatever lay at the bottom of the pit, Lynds and his team finally gave up in frustration.

Tough guy: The horned frog of Argentina will attack animals as big as a horse.

IT'S THE PITS

More treasure hunters followed. In fact, so many holes have been dug looking for the treasure that nobody knows exactly where the original hole was. Even future president Franklin D. Roosevelt supervised a dig in 1909. He was just a young man at the time but continued to follow Oak Island's progress after he became president—not that there was any success to follow. Each attempt at finding gold failed and was even more costly than the one before...which is why the hole on Oak Island became known as the "Money Pit."

KEEP OUT! THIS MEANS YOU!

Why is it so hard to get into the hole? It's no accident: Whoever dug the original pit wanted to make sure no one ever got to the bottom of it. In 1850 some explorers resting on a nearby beach noticed that the beach "gulched forth water like a sponge being squeezed." So they dug it up—and discovered the beach was *fake.* It was actually a network of stone drains that fed seawater into the Money Pit. The drains—designed to flood the pit whenever treasure hunters got too close to the treasure—had been buried in the sand to avoid detection.

It's possible that the Money Pit is also protected by poison gas. On August 17, 1965, Robert Restall, a former daredevil motorcyclist,

Tiniest tree? Greenland's two-inch tall dwarf willow.

and his 18-year-old son were attempting to seal off one of the pit's flood tunnels when Restall blacked out and fell into the hole. His son climbed down after him, but he blacked out, too. Three other workers jumped in, but to no avail—Restall, his son, and two workers were killed. Officials said they were poisoned by gas and then drowned in the water flooding the bottom of the hole.

WHAT'S BEEN FOUND IN THE HOLE?

• In 1849 three links of a gold chain were pulled up by a drill from the 98-foot level.

• In 1897 a group of drillers dug down to 155 feet. They pulled up a small square of parchment with some odd lettering on it. Could it have been part of a treasure map? The drillers were unable to find the rest of it.

• In 1976 an underwater video camera was lowered into the water-filled cavity at the bottom of the shaft. On the monitor, one of the workers suddenly saw what looked like a human hand. He quickly called over three of his crew members, and they confirmed that it truly was a hand.

• In 1987 an IBM cryptologist claimed to have deciphered the strange markings on the stone. The message: "Forty feet below, two million pounds are buried."

THE HOLE TRUTH

There are many theories as to what's really down at the bottom of the Money Pit. Here are the best known:

1. Missing crown jewels. Lots of pirates roamed the seas around Nova Scotia in the 18th century. That's when the crown jewels of the kings of France were stolen.

The Incas had no iron, so they used gold...

2. Incan gold. The treasure of the Incas was plundered by Spanish galleons and later pirated by the English buccaneer Sir Francis Drake. Wood samples from the island have been dated back to 1575, which was when Drake roamed the seas. However, there is no record of Drake ever having been to Nova Scotia.

3. Captain Kidd's buried treasure. Some believe Kidd buried his treasure on Oak Island just before he was caught by the English and hanged as a pirate. Before his death in 1701, Kidd tried to cut a

deal—he would lead the English to the spot where he'd hidden his treasure if they called off the hanging. The deal was refused, and Kidd's treasure has never been found. But there is no evidence that Kidd was ever near Oak Island.

4. The fortune of the Knights Templar. These warrior monks became very powerful after the First Crusade in 1095–1099 A.D., when they established kingdoms in Jerusalem and on the islands of Cyprus and Rhodes. Soon they had branches of their order all over Europe, controlling vast amounts of land and money. When the French king Phillip IV broke up the order and killed its leaders in the early 1300s, a few of the Templars were believed to have escaped to Scotland, where they became a secret society. A century later, they sailed to Nova Scotia and could have hidden their vast fortune on Oak Island.

...to make such everyday objects as nails, tweezers, and eating utensils.

THE SECRET REMAINS BURIED

After 200 years, the Money Pit continues to live up to its name. Since buying Oak Island in 1971, an investment group called the Triton Alliance of Montreal, Canada, has spent more than $3 million trying to uncover its secret. So far, they've retrieved…nothing.

* * *

CENTS AND NONSENSE

"Money never made a man happy yet. There is nothing in its nature to produce happiness. The more a man has, the more he wants. Instead of filling a vacuum, it makes one."

—Benjamin Franklin

"There must be more to life than having everything."

—Maurice Sendak

"Consequences, shmonsequences, as long as I'm rich."

—Daffy Duck

If the sun disappeared, it would take 8.3 minutes before the world went dark.

RECORD BREAKERS

A few more "Golden Plunger" Award winners.

FASTEST CAR: The Lamborghini Diablo 5.7. It can go from 0 to 60 miles per hour in less than four seconds and reach a top speed of more than 200 mph. That makes it the fastest "production," or mass-produced, car in the world. Cost: $250,000.

OLDEST UNIVERSITY: Université Quaraouyine in Fez, Morocco. It was founded in 859 A.D.

LONGEST BORDER BETWEEN COUNTRIES: The border between the United States and Canada. It stretches 3,987 miles (6,416 kilometers on the Canadian side of the border).

HOTTEST HOT PEPPER: The habanero. A pepper's "heat" is measured in Scoville units (named after Wilbur Scoville, a research chemist). A bell pepper has about 300, a jalepeño has about 5,000; but a habanero can have a whopping 300,000 Scoville units.

MOST EXPENSIVE MOVIE MEMORABILIA: The ruby slippers worn by Judy Garland in *The Wizard of Oz* (1939). In May 2000 they sold for a record $666,000.

SMELLIEST ANIMAL: The *zorilla*. This skunklike creature, native to Africa, protects itself by spraying a fluid from its unusually large scent glands. The stink can be smelled more than half a mile away.

BACK FROM THE DEAD

These stories prove the old adage
"It ain't over until it's over."

LUCKY JOCKEY

Early Demise: On May 8, 1936, Ralph Neves was coming down the final stretch at Bay Meadows racetrack in California when his horse tripped and crashed into the fence. The 19-year-old jockey was thrown to the ground and trampled by his own horse—and then four others. Neves was declared dead at the scene.

Still, an ambulance rushed him to a hospital where doctors tried everything they could to bring him back to life, including a shot of adrenaline directly into his heart. But nothing revived him. Finally they covered him in a sheet, tagged his toe, and sent his body off to the morgue.

I'm B-a-a-ack: Minutes after he reached the morgue, Ralph Neves sat up. He was cold, bloody, shirtless, and wearing only one boot. He wasn't sure where he was, but he knew where he was supposed to be: back at the track! So Neves staggered out of

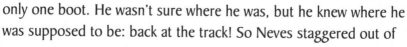

the hospital and hailed a cab.

When he got to the racetrack, he ran straight for the jockey room, still wearing his toe tag! As he sprinted past the grandstand, the crowd went wild. Then his "widow," who was still at the scene of his demise, saw him…and promptly fainted. Neves assured track officials that he didn't feel dead and was perfectly capable of riding in the next race, but they wisely convinced him to take the day off.

The next day, Neves came back to the track and rode five winners. He also claimed the day's big prize—a $500 watch donated by famed singer Bing Crosby.

DOWN BUT NOT OUT

Early Demise: April 15, 2003 was a bad day for a 10 month-old Labrador Retriever named Dosha. First, she made the mistake of wandering away from her owner's yard in Clearlake, California. Then she was hit by a car. A police officer found her and, afraid she was in too much pain, shot the pup to put her out of her misery. Her "dead" body was taken to the animal shelter and put in the freezer until the staff could bury her.

I'm B-a-a-ack: Two hours later, a veterinarian opened the freezer to find Dosha standing up in an orange plastic body bag, shivering but very much alive. This amazing dog had survived being hit by a car, shot by a bullet, and locked in a freezer. Today she's back with her family, enjoying the brand-new fence in their backyard.

OVER AND OUT

Uniform - November - Charlie - Lima - Echo
Juliet - Oscar - Hotel - November
What does it mean? Read on.

When people communicate by radio or walkie-talkie it's easy to misunderstand words, even when you spell them out letter by letter. If someone's life is on the line, mistakes can be fatal. So in the 1950s, linguists invented the NATO Phonetic Alphabet. Pilots, police and fire departments, rescue workers, and the military have used this alphabet since then to ensure their messages come through loud and clear.

A	*Alpha*		N	*November*
B	*Bravo*		O	*Oscar*
C	*Charlie*		P	*Papa*
D	*Delta*		Q	*Quebec*
E	*Echo*		R	*Romeo*
F	*Foxtrot*		S	*Sierra*
G	*Golf*		T	*Tango*
H	*Hotel*		U	*Uniform*
I	*India*		V	*Victor*
J	*Juliet*		W	*Whiskey*
K	*Kilo*		X	*X-ray*
L	*Lima*		Y	*Yankee*
M	*Mike*		Z	*Zulu*

The Snickers candy bar was named after a horse owned by the Mars family.

SEVEN ANCIENT WONDERS

Two thousand years ago, the Greeks compiled a list of the greatest structures ever built by human hands. They called them the Seven Wonders of the World. Almost all of these structures have since been destroyed, so we'll never know if they really were the greatest. But it IS a great list.

I. LIGHTHOUSE OF ALEXANDRIA. In the third century B.C., the Greeks built a huge lighthouse in the city of Alexandria, Egypt, near the Mediterranean Sea. It stood over 400 feet tall and could be seen by ships from an amazing 40 miles away! (Remember: They didn't have cranes or power tools back then.) The lighthouse overlooked the harbor for 1,600 years, until it was destroyed by an earthquake in the 14th century.

2. STATUE OF ZEUS. This massive statue was built around 450 B.C. in the Greek city of Olympia (the site of the first Olympics). Made out of ebony, ivory, gems, and a lot of gold, it depicted the Greek god Zeus seated on a throne. It was 20 feet wide by 40 feet tall. A fire destroyed it in 462 A.D.

3. TEMPLE OF ARTEMIS. Built around 550 B.C., this solid marble temple to the Greek goddess Artemis was bigger than a football field. It had 127 columns each 60 feet high and was topped by a beautifully carved roof. Inside, it was filled with precious artworks and gold and silver statues. Located in what is now Turkey, the temple stood until enemies destroyed it in 262 A.D.

4. MAUSOLEUM AT HALICARNASSUS. This was a mansion-size tomb built for King Mausolos around 353 B.C. in what is now Turkey. It became famous for its beauty and size: the alabaster and gold sarcophagus was surrounded by large columns that supported a pyramid roof—140 feet tall! An earthquake destroyed it in 1304.

5. HANGING GARDENS OF BABYLON. The Persian king Nebuchadnezzar II built this massive garden palace around 600 B.C. for Queen Amytis in what is now Iraq. Vast columned terraces on several levels were covered with full-grown trees, flowering plants, fountains, and pools. It even had several mechanically powered waterfalls. So why were the gardens called "hanging"? Historians believe it was a mistranslation of the word "overhanging." (Some historians think the gardens never really existed at all but were just a myth.)

6. COLOSSUS OF RHODES. Over 2,000 years ago, a bronze statue of the god Helios as big as the Statue of Liberty stood on the Greek island of Rhodes. The sculptor worked on it for 12 years before finally completing it in 282 B.C. It had the shortest life of any of the Seven Wonders—it was destroyed by an earthquake in 226 B.C., only 56 years after it was built.

7. THE GREAT PYRAMID. In 2560 B.C. the Egyptians built a tomb for Pharaoh Khufu. It was made with more than 2.3 million stones, each weighing more than 5,000 pounds. They were all chiseled to fit together perfectly and required no mortar. The tomb is riddled with tunnels and chambers, many still unexplored. The Great Pyramid is the only one of the Seven Wonders that remains. To this day, scientists still aren't sure how the ancient Egyptians built it.

OTHER ANCIENT WONDERS

• **Angkor Wat.** A 12th-century, 500-acre, towered and terraced Hindu temple in Cambodia.

• **Stonehenge.** A ring of huge stones—some weighing nearly fifty tons—in southern England. Construction of this sacred site spanned centuries, starting about 2950 B.C.

• **Teotihuacán.** This beautiful ancient city and temples in Mexico date back to between 200 and 650 A.D. The highlight is the Pyramid of the Sun, which is 216 feet high and covers more than 10 acres.

• **Taj Mahal.** The Mogul emperor Shah Jahan had this built as a memorial to his wife, Mumtaz Mahal, in the 1600s. The tomb itself is made of white marble inlaid with designs cut in colorful precious gems.

• **Great Wall of China.** Built 2,000 years ago to protect China from invaders, it averages 20 feet thick and 25 feet high, and is an amazing 4,500 miles long—longer than the distance from Alaska to Mexico City!

*   *   *

COW FACTS

To increase milk production, Oregon farmer Arie Jongeneel had his cows sleep on water beds. But don't laugh (at least not around the cows). Undercover investigations by the animal rights group PETA suggest that cows are humiliated when people laugh at them.

REEL SILLY

More wit than wisdom from the movies.

"I'm dishonest, and a dishonest man you can always trust to be dishonest. Honestly. It's the honest ones you want to watch out for."
—**Jack Sparrow,**
Pirates of the Caribbean

"Us elves like to stick to the four main food groups: Candy, candy canes, candy corn, and syrup."
—**Buddy the elf,** *Elf*

"It's easy to be you—I'll just suck the fun out of everything."
—**Annabel (to her mom),**
Freaky Friday

"This house is so full of people it makes me sick. When I grow up and get married, I'm living alone."
—**Kevin,** *Home Alone*

Marlin: "Okay, a mollusk walks up to this sea cucumber—well, he doesn't actually walk, he's just there—and he turns to the sea cucumber and, well... wait, there's a mollusk and a sea cucumber and..."

Chum: "You know, for a clown fish, he's not that funny."
—*Finding Nemo*

Grace: "I've got a rare blood type. I'm AB positive."

Bruce: "I'm IB positive. I be positive they ain't stickin' no needle in me."
—*Bruce Almighty*

"When I was your age, television was called books."
—**Grandpa,**
The Princess Bride

FAMILIAR NAMES

Some more people who have been
immortalized by their names.

SYLVESTER GRAHAM (1794-1851). The famous writer Ralph Waldo Emerson called Graham the "poet of bran meal and pumpkins." Why? In his day, Graham was a health and fitness advocate who recommended vegetarianism. One of his favorite snacks was named in his honor: the *graham cracker.*

ÉTIENNE DE SILHOUETTE (1709-1767). Before photography, having portraits made was expensive. So Silhouette, a French politician, made shadow portraits instead, "recommending them for their cheapness." They were named after him as a mocking tribute to his stinginess.

JOHN DUNS SCOTUS (1266-1308). In his time, Duns Scotus was a respected philosopher. But 200 years after his death, his followers, known as "Dunses," were still holding onto his out-of-date ideas. More modern thinkers criticized them for their ignorance. Eventually Dunses became *dunces.*

SAMUEL A. MAVERICK (1803-1870). Maverick was a Texas cattle baron who allowed some of his cows to roam free, without branding them first. His frustrated neighbors called these stray cows *mavericks.* The term came to include independent-minded people as well.

Big name in art: Michelangelo's last name: di Lodovico Buonarroti Simoni.

FEMALE PIRATES

Why should men get to have all the fun?

ANNE BONNEY & MARY READ

Anne Bonney was the sweetheart of pirate captain "Calico Jack" Rackham. She fought in men's clothing, had a fiery temper, and could handle a cutlass and pistol as well as any man. She often led the boarding parties during a raid.

In 1718 a tough new sailor came aboard Calico Jack's stolen ship, William, while he and Anne were raiding the Carolinas. Bonney took a fancy to the new guy but was dismayed to find out that the "guy" was actually a girl named Mary Read. But they soon became friends and, along with Jack and his crew, raided ships on the Caribbean Sea for several years.

It all came to an end in 1720 when Jack's ship was taken by surprise while captain and crew were passed out drunk in the hold. Mary and Anne tried to rally the men to fight, but it was no use— all the men were captured and sentenced to death, but the women were granted stays of execution.

Anne visited Calico Jack before his hanging. "I'm sorry to see you here," she told him, "but if you'd have fought like a man, you needn't hang like a dog."

Mary Read died of a fever in jail. As for Anne Bonney, she was released and vanished from public record. No one ever heard of her again.

Kid fact: Girls' hearts beat faster than boys' hearts.

MAGGOTS

They're not just for breakfast anymore...

GROSS QUIZ

Question: What's white or yellow, looks like a little worm, and eats garbage, rotting flesh, and animal poop? Answer: A maggot.

So what exactly *is* a maggot? It's a baby fly.

The mama fly looks for some moist, warm (usually rotten), organic matter. When she finds it, she lays her eggs in it. Then the little babies hatch, shed their skin, and turn into light-colored, half-inch-long wormy creatures that will eat anything that's organic and rotten—the smellier and more putrefied, the better. They are nature's little garbage disposals.

HEY, WE'RE THE GOOD GUYS!

Maggots break down all the dead, rotten, stinky, gross, putrid stuff in the world. They eat the poop in outhouses. They eat the rotting food and other refuse at garbage dumps. They chow down on dead animals by the side of the road. This makes them good guys. Why? They're an important part of the natural ecosystem: they help to break down the world's organic garbage so it can be absorbed back into the soil.

But maggots eat not only the rotting flesh of dead animals, but also the rotting flesh on live animals—including humans.

In the 1500s, French army doctors noticed that soldiers whose wounds were infested with maggots (*eww!*) healed faster and better than those without maggots. That started the use of *maggot*

therapy. For hundreds of years after that, doctors all over the world actually put maggots in people's wounds—on purpose! They didn't understand it, they just knew it helped. Then, in the 1940s, antibiotics and other medicines were invented and maggot therapy disappeared. But not for long…

WE'RE BACK!

In the late 1980s, researchers found a reason to begin testing maggot therapy again: antibiotics don't work for all patients. For example, Dr. Ronald Sherman in California had a patient with terrible bedsores that wouldn't heal. The patient's body was actually beginning to rot. Out of options and with nothing to lose, Dr. Sherman decided to give maggot therapy a try. He put 8,000 eggs into the sores and waited for them to hatch. When the maggots were born, they ate all the rotting flesh—but no live flesh. It worked…and the patient was healed!

Further research has found that maggots actually eat bacteria, too. They "clean" the wounds and the patients heal faster. They are especially good for treating bone infections, burns, and bed sores.

Today there are more than 1,000 clinics around the world that regularly use maggot therapy, as well as plenty of "maggot farmers" selling specially raised sterile maggots. Cheers to the maggots!

Goodnight, Shorty! People are taller in the morning than they are at night.

KID ARTISTS

Imagine someone comparing one of your paintings to work done by a famous artist. It can happen! Here are three kids who became famous artists...before they even graduated from high school.

ARTIST: Alexandra Nechita

HER STORY: Alexandra was born in Romania in 1985, then moved to the United States with her parents when she was two. Little Alex was obsessed with coloring books—so much so that her parents worried she wasn't playing enough. They stopped buying them for her, but that didn't stop Alexandra. She started drawing on any scrap of paper she could get her hands on. And when she was four, she began making her own coloring books.

When she was eight years old, Alexandra had her first solo art exhibition. Three years later, at just 11, she had become one of the most recognized artists in the world. She paints in a style called Cubism, which often shows a subject as a geometric form seen from many different angles. By the age of 15, Alexandra had achieved something most artists never do: she had earned more than $1 million. (Her work sells for $50,000 a painting.)

Pablo Picasso drew before he could talk. His first word: *lápiz*, Spanish for "pencil."

Alexandra wants to help other kids get into art, too. When recent budget cuts meant the end of art programs in many public schools, she started her own program, filling boxes with art supplies and donating them to schools. She calls it "Art in a Box." So far, Alexandra has given more than $40,000 worth of art supplies to schools in need.

ALEXANDRA SAYS: *Always believe in yourself. Feel free and never be afraid, because fear robs you of your powers and passions.*

ARTIST: George Pocheptsov

HIS STORY: George was born in Philadelphia in 1992. At the very young age of 18 months, when most kids are still learning to talk, he began teaching himself to draw. He quickly went beyond scribbles and stick figures to animals, imaginary creatures, landscapes, flowers, and portraits of his grandparents. George's whimsical style has been compared to that of Pablo Picasso or Marc Chagall, but this young artist has never had an art lesson in his life. Instead of studying art as a student at Harvard University, George concentrated on statistics, slavic languages, and literature. His paintings now sell for as much as $200,000, and he has donated more than $6 million from the sale of his art to charities.

GEORGE SAYS: *You can be anything you want. If you give up, you'll never be what you want to be, and if you don't give up, you will.*

ARTIST: Beso Kazaishvili

HIS STORY: When Beso was born in 1986, his homeland, the Republic of Georgia, was in the middle of a terrible civil war.

He began drawing when he was four years old, using burnt matchsticks. His artwork reflects the trauma of his childhood: It is full of haunting images of eyes and faces, and is painted in a style that reminds many people of the work of Spanish surrealist painter Salvador Dali.

At his first U.S. exhibition, held in California in 1998, Beso sold all of his paintings in the first half hour—33 pieces at an average price of $13,000 each! But young Beso isn't just interested in money—he is an artist with a mission. He paints so that "people will be kind to each other, so there will be no more war."

BESO SAYS: *Kids are like flowers...they close their petals and hide away when their world is full of darkness. When there is peace and love in their world, they open their petals and flood the Earth with beauty.*

THE DOG

The truth I do not stretch or shove
When I state the dog is full of love.
I've also proved, by actual test,
A wet dog is the lovingest.

—Ogden Nash

CHANGELINGS

*Most games require opponents. Here's
one you can play all by yourself.*

OBJECT OF THE GAME: To transform one word into another in
as few steps as possible.

HOW TO PLAY: Think of two contrasting words of equal length
and write them down on a piece of paper. Now, transform the first
word into the other word, changing only one letter at a time. You
must create a new word with each change each time. For example:

Dog into Cat:	Boy into Man:
dog	boy
cog	toy
cot	ton
cat	tan
	man

This was a favorite game of Lewis Carroll, who wrote *Alice in
Wonderland.* Just for fun, practice on these three Changeling
challenges by Carroll—see if you can beat him.

I. Turn Poor into Rich in 6 steps.

2. Drive Pig into Sty in 5 steps.

3. Change Tears into Smile in 6 steps.

Answers are on page 284.

If it's 0°F today and it's going to be twice as cold tomorrow, how cold will it be?

THE ALCHEMIST

In the first Harry Potter book, J. K. Rowling writes about a strange character named Nicolas Flamel. But did you know there was a real Nicolas Flamel? Here's his story.

REAL WIZARDS

A thousand years ago, *alchemists* were regarded as the leading scientific thinkers. They were the world's first chemists, carefully mixing liquids and testing metals to discover how things worked. They are often depicted as looking like wizards, with white beards and long robes, mixing magical potions. And most of them had one goal: to find the *philosopher's stone.*

A MAGICAL SUBSTANCE

What was the philosopher's stone? A giant rock where philosophers sat? A stone tablet with carved instructions? Actually, it wasn't a stone at all, but a magical powder. Alchemists believed that, taken as medicine, it could miraculously cure illnesses and even give you eternal life. Not only that, they believed the philosopher's stone held the secret to transmutation: it could magically turn any metal into gold! Alchemists thought that if they could just find the right "recipe," they could make this magical substance themselves.

So did anyone succeed in creating the philosopher's stone?

As far as we know—no. However, some people believe that at least one person did—the French alchemist, Nicolas Flamel.

A MYSTERIOUS BOOK

Nicolas Flamel's story begins in 1357 when he bought a very old, very large book in Paris. It was an unusual volume with strange drawings and engravings on its copper cover. Inside the book were 21 pages made of birch bark. Written on the first page in gold letters was the greeting: "Abraham the Jew, Priest, Prince, Levite, Astrologer, and Philosopher to the nation of the Jews dispersed by the wrath of God in France, wishes health." This prompted Flamel to call the rare volume *The Book of Abraham the Jew.*

The second page warned that only a priest or a scribe was allowed to read further—anyone else would be cursed! In the days before printing presses, a scribe was a person who copied books by hand so other people could read them. Nicolas Flamel just happened to be working as a scribe at the time, so he felt he could ignore the warnings…and read the book!

What did he find on the rest of the pages? Instructions for turning metal into gold—in other words, the *philosopher's stone*! The instructions seemed very easy to follow, except that one key piece of information was missing. The book neglected to tell the reader what kind of metal could be turned to gold.

MYSTERIOUS IMAGES

The book had many illustrations, but Flamel didn't know how to interpret them. One picture was of a young man with wings on his ankles who looked like the Roman messenger god, Mercury. Flying at him was an old man with an hourglass on his head and a scythe in his hands. Another picture was a rose bush in bloom leaning against a hollow oak tree.

Flamel showed the pictures to other people, but no one could understand them. For the next 21 years he tried to decipher the book—with no luck. At last his wife, Pernelle, suggested he try a different approach. Since it was a Jewish man who wrote the book, she said, Flamel should seek the advice of a learned Jewish scholar.

Flamel took his wife's advice and went on a long journey to find someone to help him. In Spain he met a Jewish man called Master Canches, who actually knew of the book and helped him interpret most of the pictures in it. Unfortunately, Canches died before they finished the book.

SUCCESS!

Three more years of trial and error followed. On January 18, 1382, Flamel wrote in his journal that at last he had turned mercury into silver. Three months later, he declared that he had successfully transmuted mercury to gold. "I may speak it with truth," he wrote. "I have made it three times, with the help of Pernelle who understood it as well as I because she helped me in my operations."

LOTS OF GOLD!

Did Nicolas Flamel truly discover the philosopher's stone? Did he really turn mercury into gold? No one knows for sure, but what historians do know is that Nicolas and Pernelle Flamel suddenly acquired a great deal of wealth. They founded and endowed 14 hospitals, 3 chapels, and 7 churches in Paris, and also gave to many charities. When Flamel died, he willed money and houses to even more churches and cathedrals, as well as a Paris hospital for the blind. His will, which he signed on November 22, 1416, still survives.

IMMORTALITY?

There are those who think that since Flamel discovered the secret of transmutation, he also must have discovered the secret of immortality. True believers think the Flamels went into hiding so that no one could steal the philosopher's stone from them. They claim the Flamels faked their deaths, had logs buried in their graves in the cemetery, and ran off to Switzerland.

Could they really still be alive? One thing is known for certain: their tomb is empty. Over the centuries—even into the 1900s—people have reported seeing Flamel and his wife in Switzerland, France, and India. Who knows? Nicolas and Pernelle might still be walking the streets of Paris today—very old and rich beyond belief—and all because of the philosopher's stone.

Does that mean slobs are smart? Albert Einstein was known for being messy.

WEIRD NEWS

These news stories are strange...but true!

RALPH DID IT

In April, 2004, a man in Bochum, Germany, called police to report $2,300 in damage to his car. It was covered in strange marks that wouldn't wash off. What happened? According to neighbors, someone got sick and barfed out of an apartment window...right onto the car. What made the marks? Stomach acids—they ate right through the car's paint.

FOR THE BIRDS!

Gerben Hoeksma of Holland believes that if everybody ate what he eats, world hunger would end. We'd all be healthier, too. What does he eat? Pigeon food—dried grains, peas, and seeds. It's all he's eaten for breakfast, lunch, and dinner for eleven years. He gets it at the pet store. "Since I started eating pigeon food," he says, "I've never felt so good."

DOES YOUR MAYOR TALK TO ALIENS?

Elcio Berti, mayor of Bocaiuva do Sul, Brazil, recently announced that he had scheduled a UFO landing during a local soccer game (he claims he's in regular contact with aliens). Did the spaceship come? No—the mayor changed his mind. At the last minute he contacted the aliens and told them to stay away. Why? "I was worried they might abduct one of the players."

The largest recorded snowflake was 8 inches wide.

WHERE'S THE POTTY?

More ways to ask life's most pressing question.

Afrikaans: *Waar is die toilet?*

Japanese: *Toire wa doko desu ka?*

Turkish: *Banyo nerede?*

Dutch: *Waar is het toilet?*

Norwegian: *Hvor er toalettet?*

Tagalog: *Asan ang banyo?*

Polish: *Gdzie jest toaleta?*

Danish: *Hvor er toilettet?*

Hindi: *Aapkaa snanghar kahan hai?*

Russian: *Gde zdes tualet?*

Spanish: *Donde está el baño?*

German: *Wo ist die Toilette?*

Arabic: *Ain alhamaam?*

Swedish: *Men var finns toaletterna?*

Hebrew: *Eifo hásherutim?*

Yiddish: *Vu iz der bodtsimer?*

Martian: *¤ ∂π ∆ ≈ ◊ Ω ö ∞?*

The ancient Incas harvested bat guano (poop). Why? It makes great fertilizer!

NAME THAT TUNE!

Pop quiz: What's the best-known song
in the English-speaking world?

GOOD MORNING TO YOU

In 1893 Mildred Hill wrote a little tune for her kindergarten class in Louisville, Kentucky. Her sister, Patty Hill, added some lyrics, and they had a song for teachers to sing to their students to welcome them to class. They called it "Good Morning to All," and it went like this:

> *Good morning to you,*
> *Good morning to you,*
> *Good morning dear children,*
> *Good morning to all.*

"Good Morning to All" was published in a songbook called *Song Stories for Kindergarten* and became a modest success.

IT'S A HIT!

When the songbook was reprinted in 1924, someone (to this day no one knows exactly who) changed the words "Good morning" to "Happy birthday." Result: The new version quickly became a favorite at birthday parties all over America.

The Hill sisters didn't mind that very few people knew they'd written the song—they were just happy to know that people

everywhere enjoyed it. But then it began to appear in popular movies and Broadway plays. Not only that, singers recorded hit versions of it, earning huge amounts of money and not sharing any of it with the song's composers. So in 1935 Patty Hill went to court to reclaim the rights to "Happy Birthday to You."

BIRTHDAY MONEY

She won the case easily and ever since then, whenever "Happy Birthday to You" is sung in a movie, on the stage, on radio, or on television, a sum of money—called a *royalty*—is paid to the owners of the song. (Don't worry—you don't have to pay if you sing it at a birthday party. That's free.)

Many movies and plays have birthday scenes with cakes and candles, but since it can cost thousands of dollars to use "Happy Birthday to You," actors rarely sing the Hill sisters' song. Instead, they usually sing a tune created especially for that scene.

MAKE A WISH

The Hill sisters have passed away, but their song lives on. Today "Happy Birthday to You" is owned by Warner Communications— and it still earns more than $2 million every year. That's an amazing amount of money for a simple tune made up of only six notes and six different words!

AND SPEAKING OF BIRTHDAYS...

• **Birthday cakes** have been around for only 200 years. They started in Germany, where coins and rings were baked into the cake as surprise presents.

• **Birthday cards** started in England 100 years ago. Today an estimated two billion birthday cards are mailed in the United States every year.

• **Birthday parties** were originally held for protection. It was thought that people were most vulnerable to attack by evil spirits on their birthdays, so family members and friends gathered around to keep them safe.

• **The most expensive birthday party yet** was given by the sultan of Brunei (a rich state on the island of Borneo) on July 13, 1996. It cost $27.2 million—mostly because Michael Jackson charged $16 million to perform at it.

THE CLASSIC VARIATION
(Everybody sing!)

Happy birthday to you,
You live in a zoo.
You look like a monkey,
And you smell like one, too!

*   *   *

CHEETA THE CHIMPANZEE played Tarzan's movie companion in the 1930s and 1940s, but he's famous for something else, too: At 72 years old, the *Guinness Book of World Records* named him "World's Oldest Chimp." Cheeta cheated death for another eight years, living till age 80!

FIRST LADIES

Women—and girls—haven't always had the opportunities they have today. Here's a list of some important female firsts.

FIRST FEMALE PARACHUTIST (1798): Daredevil Jeanne-Genevieve Garnerin dazzled a crowd in Paris when she leapt from a hot-air balloon and parachuted to the ground.

FIRST WOMAN AWARDED A PATENT (1809): Mary Kies was granted a patent for inventing a method of weaving straw with silk for hatmaking.

FIRST FEMALE DOCTOR (1849): Elizabeth Blackwell became the first woman to earn a medical degree in the United States. Today more than 20% of doctors and 40% of medical students are female.

FIRST FEMALE U.S. MEDAL OF HONOR WINNER (1865): Dr. Mary E. Walker received the medal for her work as a surgeon during the Civil War. She is still the only woman to have received this greatest of American military honors.

FIRST FEMALE LAWYER (1869): When Arabella Mansfield passed the Iowa bar exam, she became the first female lawyer in America. (And she did it without ever attending law school.)

FIRST FEMALE FILM DIRECTOR (1896): Alice Guy Blache made her first film only two years after Thomas Edison first demonstrated the *Kinetoscope* in Paris. Her short feature was titled *La Fée aux Choux* (*The Cabbage Fairy*). She went on to make more than 300 films in her career.

Self-made man: President Andrew Johnson was...

FIRST WOMAN TO WIN A NOBEL PRIZE (1903): Marie Curie and her husband, Pierre, won the Nobel Prize for physics for their work on radioactivity. Curie also received a Nobel Prize for chemistry in 1911, making her one of only three other scientists—male or female—to win two Nobel Prizes.

FIRST FEMALE PILOT (1908): Thérèse Peltier of France took the controls of a Voisin biplane to become the first woman to fly a plane by herself.

FIRST FEMALE POLICE OFFICER (1910): Alice Stebbins Wells, a Los Angeles social worker, petitioned the city's mayor to provide a female police officer. The petition passed and Wells was appointed as the nation's first policewoman with arrest powers.

FIRST FEMALE VETERINARIANS (1910): Elinor McGrath and Florence Kimball both graduated from veterinary school that year. Their practices were unusual because they worked only with pets (most vets at the time were horse and cattle doctors).

FIRST WOMAN IN CONGRESS (1917): Jeanette Rankin was elected to Congress from Montana. One of her first acts was to introduce a law that gave women citizenship independent of their husbands.

FIRST WOMEN TO WIN THE PULITZER PRIZE (1921): The Pulitzer is the highest award for writing in the United States. That year saw a double win for women writers. Edith Wharton won the Pulitzer prize for fiction for her book *The Age of Innocence.* Zona Gale became the first woman to win a Pulitzer for drama, for her play *Miss Lulu Bett.*

FIRST FEMALE PRIME MINISTER WORLDWIDE (1960): Sirimavo Bandaranaike became Sri Lanka's prime minister in 1960: She served three separate terms.

FIRST WOMEN IN SPACE (1963 AND 1983): Valentina Tereshkova rode into space aboard the Soviet ship Vostok 6 in 1963. Twenty years later, Sally Ride became the first American female astronaut when she orbited Earth aboard the space shuttle *Challenger* in 1983.

FIRST WOMAN TO REACH THE TOP OF MOUNT EVEREST (1975): Junko Tabei of Japan successfully climbed the world's highest mountain in 1975.

FIRST FEMALE SECRETARY OF STATE (1997): Madeleine Albright became secretary of state, the highest-ranking position ever held by a woman in the United States...so far.

*   *   *

WHAT ARE YOU AFRAID OF?

No matter what scares you, you're not alone...not even if you're scared of something as harmless as a grasshopper. Fear of grasshoppers even has a scientific name: *acridophobia.* Famous Spanish artist Salvador Dalí was so scared of the things when he was a kid, his teachers wouldn't let anyone mention them in class. And the fear didn't go away over time. At age 37, Dalí wrote, "If I were on the edge of a precipice, and a large grasshopper sprang upon me....I would prefer to fling myself over the edge than endure this frightful 'thing.'"

ODE TO A FART

This one is a real gas!

A fart can be quiet,
A fart can be loud.
Some leave a powerful
Poisonous cloud.

A fart can be short,
Or a fart can be long.
Farts have been known
To sound like a song.

A fart can create
A most curious medley.
A fart can be harmless…
Or silent but deadly.

From wide-open prairies
To small elevators,
A fart will find all of us…
Sooner or later.

So be not afraid
Of invisible gas,
And always remember
This fart, too, shall pass.

LOST CONTINENT

*You can lose your wallet. You can lose your mind.
But Uncle John wants to know—how in the
world can you lose an entire continent?*

THE LEGEND OF ATLANTIS

About 12,000 years ago—so the story goes—the noble civilization of Atlantis arose on an island continent in the Atlantic Ocean. Wise in the ways of science and the arts, its people ruled all the lands around them. The Atlanteans were so superior to the other civilizations of the day that they seemed to be superhuman, almost godlike creatures. They and their beautiful kingdom dazzled the world.

Then came a great catastrophe. A violent earthquake struck, followed by a huge tidal wave that swept across the land and destroyed Atlantis. The island, along with its temples and monuments, sank into the sea and was never seen again.

A PHILOSOPHER'S TALE

All we know of Atlantis comes from a few references in two short books, *Timaeus* and *Critias*, written by the Greek philosopher Plato around 355 B.C. Many historians think Plato was just making up a story to make a point about what happens when good governments go bad. Others disagree—they say Plato goes into far more detail than necessary for a cautionary tale. He gives very specific information about Atlantis, such as the layout of the city and its network of great canals. According to Plato, Atlantis was destroyed 9,000 years before his time.

Deepest ocean: the Mariana Trench, in the Pacific Ocean is 36,201 feet deep.

Plato called his story a "genuine history" within "the realm of fact." But was it? That question has haunted peoples' imaginations ever since. Thousands of books have been written about Atlantis. Hundreds of expeditions have combed every corner of the globe, searching for traces of the fabled lost continent—yet no proof of its existence has ever been found.

WHERE IN THE WORLD

So, if Atlantis was a real place, where would it have been? Plato said it was located on an island "west of the Pillars of Hercules." The Pillars of Hercules is an ancient name for the rocky outcroppings at the east end of the Strait of Gibraltar, a narrow channel of water dividing Europe from Africa and connecting the Mediterranean Sea with the Atlantic Ocean. In ancient times, the Pillars of Hercules were considered by Mediterranean peoples to be the edge of the known world. Few ships ventured beyond them.

Lying due west of the Pillars of Hercules are the Azores Islands. Early Atlantis seekers assumed these lonely islands were all that was left of the mountain peaks of Atlantis. But geological surveys of the Atlantic Ocean floor show that it is covered with a very thick layer of mud that took millions of years to accumulate. There's no sign of a sunken island.

ANOTHER THEORY

If Atlantis isn't in the Atlantic Ocean, then where?

In 1909 a history professor named K. T. Frost came up with one of the likeliest possibilities. Instead of going west from ancient Greece, Professor Frost suggested, go east. And what if Atlantis was destroyed not 9,000 years but only *900* years before Plato's time? Making these two changes to the story puts Atlantis in a place that was very well-known to the ancient Greeks: the island of Crete, 60 miles southeast of the mainland.

Today Crete is part of Greece, but it was once home to the Minoan Empire, a great civilization that ruled the Mediterranean for hundreds of years before the Greeks did. The Minoans were far more sophisticated than their Greek neighbors. They had great palaces filled with beautiful paintings, a highly organized government, and a powerful navy. Their code of laws even gave women the same legal status as men, something that is taken for granted in many cultures today, but which was uncommon 3,000 years ago.

Then, at its very height, the Minoan civilization vanished almost overnight.

Thar She Blows!

To this day no one knows for sure what happened, but we do know of one natural disaster that might explain a lot. About 70 miles from Crete lies the island of Thera. It's actually several small islands ringing a central lagoon, but 3,500 years ago it was all one big island with a volcano at its center. Around the year 1500 B.C.—almost 900 years before Plato's time—it blew up.

Ash thrown up into the atmosphere would have blackened the skies for days, and the sound of the explosion could have been heard thousands of miles away. But the most lethal effect of the eruption would have been the tidal wave it created. Probably over 100 feet tall, the wave would have swept more than a mile

A *junk* is a sailing ship commonly seen in China, Indonesia, and India.

inland and drowned the Minoan cities before anyone had a chance to escape. The powerful Minoan navy would have been sunk in minutes and the great island empire completely destroyed.

GONE BUT NOT FORGOTTEN

Assuming Plato really did make mistakes in his dates and his directions, the Minoan theory is the most accepted one proposed about the fate of Atlantis.

But there are other theories. One says that the great city was indeed in the Atlantic Ocean, but much farther away—off the coast of Florida in the area known today as the Bermuda Triangle. Others put the lost continent back in the Mediterranean, near the island of Cyprus. And the most extreme theory places Atlantis in the South China Sea off the coast of Vietnam.

Some 2,500 years and 25,000 books later, the debate rages on with no end in sight. The only clear truth about the lost continent is that very few stories have held such a lasting grip on the human imagination as has Atlantis.

*　　*　　*

From *The Eskimo Cookbook*, 1952
"Do not make loon soup."

The first helicopter (1907) flew for 20 seconds and was just a foot off the ground.

SNOT RAGS

What did people use before Kleenex?

ON THE NOSE

Handkerchiefs first appeared more than 2,000 years ago in Rome. These early hankies—called *sudaria*—were used mostly to wipe sweat from a person's face or hands. They were made of linen, which was expensive at the time, so only the very rich could afford them.

But as linen making spread across Europe, more and more people began carrying handkerchiefs. The first recorded mention of using a cloth to blow one's nose dates from 300 A.D. Before that the preferred method was what's known as a *farmer's blow*: press a finger against one nostril to close it, and blow hard through the other. The handkerchief made it possible to keep a clear nose and be polite about it.

By the 1300s, many people carried hankies, often tucked inside their sleeves. Great time and expense were spent creating lace and embroidered handkerchiefs so beautiful that people didn't want to use them as snot rags. Many folks preferred to use their sleeves rather than goober up their lace hankies.

King Francis I of France found the habit disgusting, so in the 1500s, he decreed that buttons were to be sewn on men's coat sleeves to remind them to use their handkerchiefs for blowing their noses. The buttons turned into a fashion statement that continues today.

What? Bees don't have ears.

MONSTER MATCH

Do you know a chupacabra from a banshee? Take this quiz to see if you can match the monster's name with its description.

I. If you hear the scream of this nasty Irish demon in the middle of the night, it means that someone will die…soon!

  a) Banshee **b)** Methuselah **c)** Gremlin

2. This one-eyed giant from Greece will eat anything, including people. Fortunately, he's really stupid, so it's easy to get away from him.

  a) Chupacabra **b)** Ganesh **c)** Cyclops

3. This evil spirit from the Middle East robs graves and lives off the flesh of the dead.

  a) Gideon **b)** Ghoul **c)** Gruyère

4. This half-human, half-monster from Arabia likes to hide in brass lamps. Rub the lamp three times and you'll get three wishes.

  a) Borg **b)** Pan **c)** Jinn

5. Its name means "knocking ghost" in German. It loves to break dishes, turn lights on and off, and send furniture crashing across the room.

  a) Poltergeist **b)** Yeti **c)** Mr. Tidball

Folk remedy: Put a Bible under your pillow to keep from having nightmares.

6. A corpse that's been brought back to life by voodoo magic or witchcraft, this monster comes from the West Indies and walks the Earth in a robotlike trance.

a) Mummy   **b)** Zombie   **c)** Brainiac

7. This bloodsucker from Transylvania always avoids the light of day. He'll live forever unless a wooden stake is driven through his heart.

a) Werewolf   **b)** Troll   **c)** Vampire

8. A wicked winged creature from Latin America. This monster has lizardlike skin, a row of spikes down its back, red eyes, huge fangs, long claws, and a bad temper.

a) Chupacabra   **b)** Poltergeist   **c)** Goblin

9. First discovered by British pilots during WWII, this little dude with the big ears loves to wreak havoc on machines and appliances. If you smash your thumb with a hammer, this is the monster to blame.

a) Leprechaun   **b)** Swamp Thing   **c)** Gremlin

10. This ugly giant stays deep inside the mountains of Scandinavia and Germany but also likes to live under bridges. He's almost indestructible, but expose him to sunlight and he'll turn to stone… or explode.

a) Sasquatch   **b)** Troll   **c)** Uncle John (Hey!)

Answers

1. a; 2. c; 3. b; 4. c; 5. a; 6. b; 7. c; 8. a; 9. c; 10. b

WHO WAS LEONARDO?

You may know that Leonardo da Vinci painted the Mona Lisa, possibly the world's most famous painting. But did you know he was also a musician, a scientist, an inventor, and an engineer?

RENAISSANCE MAN

Leonardo da Vinci was born in Italy in 1452 and lived during the period of world history now known as the Renaissance, which means "rebirth." It was a time when many brilliant thinkers made breakthroughs in art, mathematics, and science. But Leonardo could do it all. He was so good at so many things that he became the model for what we now call a *Renaissance man*—someone who excels at everything he tries.

Painter

As a 14-year-old boy in Florence, he was apprenticed to the famous artist Andrea del Verrocchio, but he quickly became better than his teacher. Leonardo's landscapes transformed art. He found that he could create a sense of depth in his paintings by imitating the way the air blurs distant objects.

Last Supper and *The Virgin of the Rocks* are two of his best-known paintings, but he is most famous for his painting of the mysterious smiling woman known as the Mona Lisa.

That's nutty! Peanuts are fruits, not nuts.

Code Writer

Leonardo da Vinci was ambidextrous and a good multitasker: he could draw a sketch with one hand and write a letter with the other hand *at the same time*. And when he wanted to keep something a secret, he wrote backward, from right to left. You need a mirror to read his writing.

Anatomical Artist

Leonardo studied anatomy by dissecting corpses, and created a method of drawing human anatomy that is still used by medical artists today. He developed the technique of drawing cross-sections to show the inside of the head. And when he drew organs that lay on top of each other, he made the ones in front appear transparent.

Engineer

At age 30, Leonardo wrote to the duke of Milan, who had an immense army equipped with the most modern weapons available at the time. Leonardo told him that he had studied all the latest "machines of war" and had come up with many improvements. He had designs for cannons, mortars, catapults, portable bridges, and armored vehicles. He wrote that he was able to "dry up the water of the moats" during sieges, destroy fortresses, and dig tunnels under walls and even under rivers. Modesty was not one of Leonardo's qualities: in the same letter, he told the duke that he was a master of architecture, could sculpt in marble, bronze, and clay, and could paint "as well as any man, whoever he be." The letter worked. The duke brought Leonardo to Milan and became his patron.

The Sahara Desert in Africa is almost as big as the United States.

Musician and Theatrical Designer

Leonardo played an early version of the violin, and designed and built them for others. For special events, he directed pageants, designed intricate sets and costumes, and even chose the music. For parties, he created mechanical robots that would open and shoot out fireworks.

Scientist

Leonardo has been called the first modern scientist. He filled hundreds of notebooks with his sketches of and theories about nature. His careful observation of the movement of water, the flight of birds, and the speed of light and sound led him to some remarkable conclusions. For example, Leonardo was the first to see that it was the movement of air over a bird's wing—not just its flapping—that gave it lift, an observation that wouldn't be understood by science for another 300 years. He also made discoveries in meteorology and geology, and even learned the effect of the moon on the tides.

Inventor

Leonardo da Vinci's notebooks are crammed with cartoons, sketches for new paintings, even descriptions of what he had for lunch. But his genius is most obvious in the mind-boggling inventions he dreamed up—everything from a submarine to a flying machine.

His motto was, "No obstacle will stop me," and he lived by it. He was curious about the world around him and never stopped gathering information. His final years were spent with the king of

Albert Einstein, Leonardo da Vinci, and Mr. Rogers were all vegetarians.

France, who wanted nothing more than to talk with him. When Leonardo died at the age of 67, the king declared, "I do not believe that there has ever been a man born into the world who knew as much as Leonardo."

*   *   *

LEONARDO'S DESIGNS

Most of Leonardo's inventions were not built during his lifetime because they were too advanced for the technology of his day. Here are some of the designs found in his notebooks:

- Alarm clock
- Robot
- Contact lenses
- Ball bearings
- Shoes for walking on water
- Compass
- Crane
- Pedometer
- Diving bell
- Eyeglasses
- Gas mask
- Helicopter

- Air conditioner
- Parachute
- Steam engine
- Pliers
- Revolving stage
- Screw-making machine
- One-person battleship
- Tank
- Telescope
- Water turbine
- Multibarreled machine gun
- Self-closing toilet lid

Real title of Leonardo da Vinci's famous painting, the Mona Lisa: *La Gioconda*.

PALINDROMES

Palindromes are words or sentences that are spelled the same way backward or forward. Here are some of our favorites.

Not a banana baton.

Put Eliot's toilet up.

Pull up, Bob, pull up.

Wanna tan? Naw.

If I had a hi-fi…

Don't nod.

Won't I? No stats on it now.

Egad! Alas! A salad age.

May a moody baby doom a yam?

I, madam, I made radio! So I dared! Am I mad? Am I?

No lemons, no melon.

Name now one man.

Gnu dung.

Was it a rat I saw?

Draw, O coward!

Did Mom poop? Mom did.

Now Eve, we're here, we've won.

Ten animals I slam in a net.

Cigar? Toss it in a can. It is so tragic.

No, son.

Mr. Owl ate my metal worm.

Emil, a sleepy baby, peels a lime.

Some men interpret nine memos.

UFO tofu.

Waaaaaaaah! The average newborn baby spends 113 minutes a day crying.

CRAZY TEACHERS

*Teachers are supposed to set a good example for
kids. So what were these guys thinking?*

FLYING SCHOOL

In March, 2004, a student at Miami Beach High School asked
permission to jump out of the 2nd floor classroom window—and
the teacher let him! Not only that, he bet the student $20 that he
couldn't do it without being injured. Bad idea: The teacher lost the
$20 (the student was uninjured)...and his job.

ACT YOUR AGE

In 1995 Winchester Elementary in Memphis, Tennessee, held a
special dance to reward students for their good behavior. When
the dance was over, two teachers got into an argument: one told
the kids to wait inside by the door; the other told them to go
outside. How did they resolve their differences? By punching and
hitting each other. Result: Both teachers were fired for their bad
behavior—at the good-behavior dance.

IS THIS BEING TAPED?

In 2004 a 14-year-old student was misbehaving at Oran Elementary
School in Missouri. How did the teacher handle it? She duct-taped
his hands, arms, and legs to his desk and taped his mouth shut.
When his father complained that the boy had "nearly suffocated,"
the teacher, a 21-year veteran, was forced to resign.

TREE SNORKELING

*No, it's not a Dr. Seuss story—it's a new sport
that takes tree climbing to the extreme.*

BARKING UP THE RIGHT TREE

Using gear borrowed from rock climbers and a crossbow (we'll tell you why in a second), scientists, researchers, moms, dads, sisters, and brothers all over the world are going out on a limb, literally. They're climbing trees—*serious* trees, more than 200 feet tall and 400 years old.

LEARNING THE ROPES

The crossbow is used to shoot an arrow with a length of fishing line attached over the lowest branch of the tree, which is often 100 feet off the forest floor. The climbing rope, which is tied to the other end of the fishing line, is then pulled up over the branch.

Once the rope is anchored, the climber climbs up by using two *ascenders*, which clamp around the rope. The ascenders slide upward easily but lock in place so they won't slide down. With one ascender attached to a stirrup and the other attached to a sling (you sit in the sling), a tree climber goes up the rope like an inchworm: stand up…sit down…stand up…sit down…again and again until reaching the branch. Really tall trees may require you to repeat the whole process several times.

BRANCHING OUT

Tree climbers say that something weird happens when they climb a really tall tree: Time slows down. The air becomes brilliant. The forest sounds are sharper. The tree they're climbing seems to whisper to them. This is *tree time.* They're in "the zone" with the tree, and it's a feeling that all tree climbers love.

Before you know it, you've gone as high as you can go. The branches above are too thin to hold your weight. The people on the forest floor below look like dolls. Time to go back down? No way! Now it's time to take a snooze in your "treeboat." Treeboats are hammocks equipped with stabilizers and anchors that keep the climber safely tucked inside.

Coming down the tree can be just as fun as ascending. You rappel down like a rock climber, using your feet to bounce off the side of the trunk all the way to the ground. Then it's time to retrieve the climbing rope and find a new, taller tree!

TREE-CLIMBING TERMS

Tree surfing: When a tree climber encounters strong winds, the tree begins to sway. Each gust of wind is like a huge wave, swinging you and the tree back and forth. Before long, the whole forest is rippling with the wind. Now you're tree surfing.

Tree snorkeling: That's when you move from one tree to another without coming back down to the ground (picture Tarzan with a lot of safety gear). Scientists and researchers studying the health and biodiversity of the forest canopy use tree-snorkeling techniques to save "down time"—time on the forest floor or time lost while climbing.

Bark bite: The nickname for the scrapes you get when you rub up against a tree. Like a vertical road rash, only the road is the tree bark.

Ninja climbs: Sneaky climbing…when the forest rangers aren't looking.

Tree dandruff: The bits of bark and lichen that fall through the canopy when they're dislodged by climbers.

Ready to try your hand (and feet) at tree snorkeling?
Turn to the Resource Guide on page 285.

"We are what we pretend to be."
—**Kurt Vonnegut Jr.**

Are they nuts? The pecan is the official state tree of Texas.

UNCLE SAM

Uncle John wants YOU...to read this article!

SAM I AM

People sometimes refer to the United States or its government as "Uncle Sam." And Uncle Sam—a tall, white-haired man with a beard, dressed in striped pants and top hat—has become a national symbol. But was there ever a real Uncle Sam? You bet.

His name was Sam Wilson. He didn't have a white beard, and he never wore striped pants, but he did wear a top hat. He was a meat supplier for American troops during the War of 1812. Meat sent to the army was stamped with the initials "U.S.," for United States, which meant it had passed inspection and was fit to eat.

One day a meat inspector came into Sam Wilson's shop. As he stamped the approved cuts with "U.S.," a worker joked that the letters stood for "Uncle Sam," Wilson's nickname. The joke caught on and soon all government supplies sent to the troops were said to be from "Uncle Sam."

That's the legend...but is it true? In 1961, someone found an 1830 newspaper article quoting a soldier who happened to be in Wilson's store when the employee joked about the initials. That was enough to convince Congress, and they issued a proclamation declaring Sam Wilson to be the country's original Uncle Sam.

Q: What do Eskimo Pies, Ovaltine, and Aquafresh toothpaste...

NAVEL GAZING

At last you have an excuse to stare at your belly button.

BELLY BUTTON ANALYSIS

Dr. Gerhard Reibmann, a psychologist from Germany, believes your belly button can tell your personality type. In his book, *Understanding Yourself through Your Navel*, he says that there are six types of belly buttons. Which one do you have?

1. Horizontal Navel: This type is oblong and spreads sideways across the stomach. People with horizontal navels are complex, multifaceted, and highly emotional.

2. Vertical Navel: If your belly button stretches up and down, it shows that you are a self-confident person who is generous and emotionally stable.

3. Outie: This belly button sticks out. It reveals an optimistic person who embraces life with enthusiasm.

4. Innie: If your belly button is bowl-shaped or concave, it means you are gentle, loving, and sensitive, but prone to worry. People with innies are delicate.

5. Off-Center Navel: An off-center belly button indicates a fun-loving, unusual individual who experiences big highs and big lows.

6. Round Navel: This belly button is evenly shaped and round. If you have one of these, it means you are even-tempered with a quiet, retiring personality.

7. No Navel: You're an alien!

GROOVY GROUNDHOGS

*Your mom won't let you get a dog? Maybe
you can talk her into a pet groundhog...*

WOODY WOODCHUCK

Groundhogs (also called woodchucks) live in the eastern and midwestern United States and Canada. These animals are about the size and weight of an adult cat, with small, round ears and black eyes and nose. They have coarse gray fur on their upper parts and yellowish orange fur on their underparts.

Groundhogs love to burrow. In the wild, these furry creatures are usually found in their tunnels underground. Fruits and vegetables are their favorite foods, which is why they're often caught in people's gardens and why they've made the official pest list.

But not everyone thinks of them as outdoor pests—some people actually keep them indoors as pets.

BASIC TRAINING

Like cats, groundhogs are fussy about staying clean and can be trained to use a litter box. Their teeth and claws must be kept trimmed—otherwise they'll do the trimming themselves on your furniture and carpets. They can be very loving and playful but need plenty of exercise and cannot live in a cage. Since groundhogs live to dig, it's a good idea to provide them with a way to do that, or they might dig a hole through your floor!

Groundhogs are hibernating animals, so they tend to doze a lot in the winter. That means you don't have to worry about entertaining them, but on the other hand, they can get lonely and long for a mate.

Most animal experts don't recommend keeping a wild animal as a pet, but there are breeders who raise groundhogs for that purpose (some states require you to license your groundhog just like a dog). In captivity, groundhogs can live to be 10 years old, and people who have pet groundhogs say they are as cute and lovable as any family cat.

And speaking of groundhogs, here's the story of...

GROUNDHOG DAY

February 2 is the midpoint between *winter solstice* (when the sun is farthest south) and *vernal equinox* (the first day of spring, when night and day are the same length). It has been celebrated for centuries as a sign that soon it will be time for farmers to plant their crops.

The Germans had a planting superstition centered around badgers. If a badger saw its shadow when it came out of hibernation, that meant more winter was to come and planting should be put off for a few weeks. If it didn't see its shadow, warm weather was on its way and planting could begin. When German settlers came to Pennsylvania in the 1700s, they found no badgers,

Yum! Seventy-five percent of the world's maple syrup comes from Canada.

but lots of hibernating groundhogs, so they switched animals and created Groundhog Day.

In the 1880s, a group of friends in Punxsutawney, Pennsylvania, went into the woods on February 2 to look for groundhogs. This outing became an annual tradition, and a local newspaper editor nicknamed the seekers the Punxsutawney Groundhog Club. By 1887 the search had become an official event and the groundhog had been named Punxsutawney Phil.

Phil 'er Up!

There have been lots of Phils over the years. Today the official Phil is a pet groundhog who lives in a climate-controlled habitat next to the Punxsutawney Library. Phil was already famous in Pennsylvania, but in 1993 the movie *Groundhog Day* made him a national star. Crowds gather every February 2 to watch Phil come out of his burrow and look for his shadow.

There are other cities that have their own fuzzy-faced celebrities. New York City's groundhog is called Pothole Pete. Even Canada has its own groundhog, an albino named Wiarton Willie. But when it comes to predicting the end of winter, Punxsutawney Phil is still considered top hog.

COOKING WITH UNCLE JOHN

Instead of swallowing bicycle chains and skateboard parts like Mr. Eat-It-All (see page 53), try this tasty recipe.

EDIBLE GLASS

You will need:
9-by-13-inch baking sheet
Nonstick frying pan
Large wooden spoon
Help from a grown-up

Ingredients:
1 tablespoon butter
1 cup sugar
Food coloring for making "stained glass" (optional)

1. Butter the baking sheet and put it in the refrigerator.

2. Put the sugar in the frying pan. Ask a grown-up to help while you cook the sugar on low heat. Stir slowly with the wooden spoon. As the sugar begins to melt, it will start to turn light brown and stick together. Continue stirring until it melts into a thick brown liquid.

3. Add a few drops of food coloring, if you like.

4. Pour the melted sugar onto the cold baking sheet. Let it cool. The melted sugar will harden into a sheet of edible "glass." Yum! Sure beats nails, doesn't it?

DUNE RIDERS

The snow has melted. The skate park is too crowded. What's a kid to do? Grab a board and head for the desert!

SANDBOARDING

There's a new sport in town: Sandboarding. It's a lot like snowboarding, only you don't have to wait for cold weather. And you can *bomb the hill, carve, catch air,* and do tricks, just like on snow.

According to historians, the ancient Egyptians went "boarding" on the sand dunes of northern Africa using large pieces of pottery. Americans and Brazilians have been doing it since the 1950s, using everything from pieces of cardboard to old car hoods.

THE BOARD

A modern sandboard looks a lot like a snowboard: it's long and narrow with foot straps on the top and a little rocker on the plank. But there is a difference. The bottom of the sandboard is flat for maximum surface contact, and the sides scoop upward slightly to prevent digging into the sand. The biggest difference, however, is in the board's composition: snowboards are usually made from polyethylene—a sandboard is made from an extra-slick material, such as Formica.

Don't have a sandboard? Don't worry—you can use an old snowboard. It might ride a bit slower, so if you want to speed it up, wax the bottom with sandboard wax. Other waxes will slow you down, ruin the board, and damage the environment (sand waxes are Teflon- or soy-based).

In 1984 Jack Smith crossed the United States in 26 days...on a skateboard.

WHERE CAN YOU BOARD?

• Go to an ocean beach or a desert. Check out the shores of lakes. Just about any dune will do as long as it's dry sand—wet sand makes the board stick.

• Look for clean dunes with sandy bottoms. You don't want to end your run in the rocks! Make sure there are no pieces of glass, cans, sticks, driftwood, or buried fire pits in the dunes.

• Beginners need dunes that are not too steep. Many dunes are 500 feet tall or more, and a sandboarder coming down can reach speeds over 40 miles per hour. So make sure you get the hang of it before you start trying to catch the big air.

DOES IT HURT WHEN YOU FALL?

Think about it—a face-plant ending with a mouthful of sand? *Ouch!* That's why you want those newbie dunes when you're starting out. Wear sunscreen, a helmet, and durable clothing— no reason to get a sand rash.

Ready to ride? Have fun, and remember: there's no shame in riding sitting down. Now, go find a dune, step on your board, buckle up the bindings—and don't stop until you get to the bottom.

Want to find a sandboarding park? Surf over
to the Resource Guide on page 285.

Volleyball was invented in 1895.

I SAW
THE POTATO

More advertising blunders from doing business abroad.

KENTUCKY FRIED CHICKEN. When KFC's slogan "Finger-lickin' good" was translated into Chinese, it came out as "Eat your fingers off."

SCHWEPPES TONIC WATER. In Italy, a campaign for Schweppes Tonic Water translated the name into Schweppes *Toilet Water*.

PEPSI. The Pepsi slogan "Come alive with the Pepsi Generation" was mistranslated in Taiwan to say, "Pepsi will bring your ancestors back from the dead."

T-SHIRTS. When the Pope came to the States for a visit, an American T-shirt maker in Miami printed shirts for the Spanish-speaking market that were supposed to declare, "I saw the Pope." Instead they announced, "I saw the Potato."

Napoleon was afraid of cats.

MONSTER GIGGLES

Uncle John likes monsters. He also likes jokes. And he thinks these monster jokes are abominable...er, horrible...er, great!

Q: What do you get if you cross the Abominable Snowman with a kangaroo?
A: *A fur coat with pockets.*

A police officer stopped a man walking a monster and ordered him to take it to the zoo. The next day the officer saw the same man, still with the monster.

"I told you to take that monster to the zoo," he said.

"I did," said the man. "Now I'm taking it to the movies."

Q: What do you call a dog owned by Dracula?
A: *A bloodhound.*

Q: Where does a vampire take a bath?
A: *In a bat-tub.*

Q: What did the grandfather monster say to his grandson when they hadn't seen each other for a while?
A: *You gruesome!*

Q: What do vampire sailors call their ships?
A: *Blood vessels.*

A very snobbish man was in an art gallery, when he stopped by one particular exhibit.

"I suppose this picture of a hideous monster is what you call modern art," he sniffed.

"No, sir," replied the assistant, "that's what we call a mirror."

Q: How do you keep a curious monster in suspense?
A: *I'll tell you tomorrow.*

Animal fact: Octopi have three hearts.

HOT DAWGS

If they ever let animals compete in the
Olympics, watch out for these guys!

TAIL-WAGGERS

St. Bernards love snow. For centuries these big shaggy dogs have worked to rescue avalanche victims and snowbound hikers. But there's a pair in northern Japan who'd rather hit the slopes on skis. Colt and Lucky live with the Sato family. Most mornings, the Satos take the dogs up the mountain and help them into their specially made boots, bindings, and skis. Then the two St. Bernards go wooshing down the slopes. There's only one little problem: the dogs don't know how to stop, so Colt and Lucky always ski on a leash.

KNUCKLE-DRAGGER

Louie the chimpanzee is a movie star. His film credits: *MVP: Most Valuable Primate* (he was an ice hockey player) and *MVPII: Most Vertical Primate* (he was a skateboarder). After all that training, learning how to snowboard for his third movie, *MXP: Most Extreme Primate*, was a piece of cake. Louie started out on a carpeted treadmill, but he was shredding the snow after just eight weeks of training. As his trainer says, "They call boarders knuckle-draggers, so he fits right in." Like all little kids, Louie occasionally stops to eat the snow. (Anyone tell him to stay away from the yellow stuff?)

On Feb. 18, 1979, it snowed in the Sahara Desert, but only for 30 minutes.

T E BEAN CA

No, it's not just an excuse to make another joke about gas—this car was really made out of beans.

BACKGROUND

Henry Ford had lots of big ideas. In 1913 he came up with his biggest: using an assembly line to build cars. Cars would no longer be handmade one at a time, they'd be mass-produced hundreds at a time. Even after the assembly line was up and running, Ford kept trying to find cheaper and more efficient ways to build his cars.

Although he is known as one of history's greatest industrialists, Ford was raised on a farm. From this upbringing, he developed a lifelong interest in putting science to work for agriculture. In 1929 he built a laboratory to research potential new uses for farm crops, especially one crop in particular: soybeans.

PLASTIC RAP

Today, about half of the items we use in our daily lives are made from plastic. But in the 1930s, plastic was the new miracle product. Combs, brushes, buttons, and jewelry were just starting to be made out of the stuff. Ford wondered if cars could be made out of plastic, too.

Most of the plastic we use today is derived from hydrocarbons, such as petroleum oil. But it can also be made from any carbon-based fiber, which means almost any plant. Knowing this, in 1932 Ford called his scientists together in Detroit, dumped a few bags of soybeans on the floor, and said, "You fellows are supposed to be a bunch of smart guys. See what you can make out of these."

Smallest motorized car ever? The Denso Micro-Car. It's the size of a grain of rice.

Two years later, the Ford team came up with a soybean oil that they used to make a tough enamel for painting cars. They also developed a soybean paste that could be molded into car horn buttons. By 1940 two pounds of soybeans were going into every Ford car as gearshift knobs, door handles, pedals, and gears. His labs also came up with a new, improved plastic that was 10 times stronger than steel—but weighed a third less.

BEAN MACHINE

Ford wanted to start making car doors and hoods out of this amazing new material, but first he had to convince a skeptical public. He called in a group of reporters, then jumped up and down on a sheet of his new soybean plastic. It didn't bend an inch. "If that was steel," Ford declared, "it would have caved in."

In 1941 Henry Ford finally built the first soybean car. It was a sensation! People marveled at the tough soybean plastic body and the clear plastic windows and windshield. The seats were upholstered in a soybean "wool." The only metal in the car body was in its frame, which meant the car weighed less than a regular car—1,000 pounds less. Newspapers all over the country raved about it and predicted that soon every new car would be made out of plastic.

STOPPED SHORT

But it all came to screeching halt when the Japanese attacked Pearl Harbor on December 7, 1941. Suddenly the United States was at war, and Ford and the other carmakers had to convert their factories from making cars to building new steel tanks, jeeps,

planes, ships, and submarines for the armed forces. No new cars were made until after World War II ended in 1945. By that time Ford had moved on to other projects, and the soybean car was forgotten.

BACK TO THE FUTURE

When Henry Ford started experimenting with soybeans back in the 1930s, he said, "Soybeans will make millions of dollars for farmers, and provide us with needed things nobody even knows about now." It turns out that Ford was ahead of his time. Today soybeans are one of America's biggest cash crops and the country's most valuable export. They're used in plastics, but you'll also find them in inks, varnishes, paints, and glues…and new Ford cars.

In 2003 the Ford company celebrated its 100th anniversary by building a new bean car, or more accurately, a "veggie" car. The roof and carpet mats of the new Model U are made from corn; the seats and bumpers are made from soybeans; and the oil used to lubricate the engine comes from sunflower seeds. Plus there's no dirty exhaust—instead of smoke, the hydrogen-powered engine gives off steam. And this car of the future is almost totally biodegradable!

Mr. Bean: Henry Ford once went to a convention wearing clothes made from soybeans.

MORE "LONGESTS"

Are you longing for another good read? Try this page.

• **LONGEST ALPHABET:** The Cambodian alphabet has 74 letters (English has 26).

• **LONGEST PRO BASEBALL GAME:** The Chicago White Sox and Milwaukee Brewers played a game on May 9, 1984, that lasted 8 hours, 6 minutes. The White Sox won in the 25th inning, 7–6.

• **LONGEST MIGRATION:** The Arctic tern flies from the Arctic to the Antarctic and back every year—a round trip of 25,000 miles.

• **LONGEST-LIVING INSECT:** The wood-boring beetle of Ecuador has a lifespan of 45 years.

• **LONGEST DINOSAUR:** From fossilized bone fragments found in 1991, scientists estimate that the seismosaurus was 150 feet long.

• **LONGEST LIMOUSINE:** Jay Ohrberg of California built one that measures 100 feet. It has 26 wheels and is hinged in the middle so it can turn corners.

• **LONGEST WORD IN THE ENGLISH LANGUAGE:** *Pneumonoultramicroscopicsilicovolcanoconiosis.* It has 45 letters and is the name of a lung disease.

• **LONGEST DANCE:** Mike Ritof and Edith Boudreaux won a dance marathon contest when they danced for 5,154 hours and 48 minutes, from August 29, 1930, to April 1, 1931. Their prize: $2,000.

• **LONGEST SCHOOL YEAR:** Chinese students attend school 251 days of the year (U.S. average: 180).

• **LONGEST SOFA:** Italian furniture maker Industrie Natuzzi made a red leather sofa in 2001 that was 115 feet, 2 inches long. It took more than 50 cow hides to cover it.

• **LONGEST CITY NAME:** This honor goes to Bangkok, the capital city of Thailand. Its full name is 165 letters long: *Krung Thep Mahanakhon Amarn Ratanakosin Mahintharayutthaya Mahadilok Phob Noparatratchathani Burirom Udomratchanivetmahasathan Amornpan Avatarnsathit Sakkathattiyavisnukarmprasit.* What's it all mean? "City of Angels."

• **LONGEST SNEEZING FIT:** Donna Griffiths of Pershore, England, first sneezed on January 13, 1981, and didn't stop until September 16, 1983. That's 978 days! She sneezed an estimated one million times in the first year alone. (*Gesundheit!*)

*   *   *

Sci-fi author Ray Bradbury loved the word *ramshackle*. Why? "Half the time we feel we are ramshackle people, lopsided, no right or left side of the brain, with some terrible vacuum in between."

PIRATE STYLE

*Aaaargh! Avast ye, matey! 'Ere's me pirate
stuff. Now, choose yer weapons!*

THE PIRATE'S ARMORY

Pirates earned their living by robbing ships. Most merchant crews
would give up the minute they saw the Jolly Roger—the famous
flag with a skull and crossbones—flying from the mast of the
pirate ship. After all, they had no desire to die for the rich man
who owned the ship and cargo. Sometimes, though, crews would
resist—and the pirates would attack. These were the pirates'
weapons of choice:

Cutlass. The sword of the seas. Shorter than a saber or
sword, and usually curved. Designed for hacking, not
thrusting. Every pirate had one.

Dagger. A small knife essential to fighting with a cutlass.
They were used to block an opponent's sword or to give a
killing thrust when the opponent's guard was down.

Pistol. Pirates kept their pistols stuffed in their belts and used
them for clubs after firing the single bullet. Pirate captains
often used pistols, elaborately engraved on the handles and
barrels, as bribes to get their men to form boarding parties
against enemy ships. Why? Because leading a boarding party
was dangerous! It took a strong incentive—like a beautiful
new pistol—to get someone to do it.

Sir Barks-a-lot: In medieval Europe, some dogs wore suits of armor.

Blunderbuss. A short, blunt, shotgunlike musket that was more of a cannon than a rifle. With its deafening roar and ability to spray lead shot all over the deck, nothing beat a blunderbuss for repelling an onslaught.

Marlinespike. The favored weapon of mutineers. Because sailors and pirates were prone to rebellion, all weapons on board a ship would be stored in the armory and handed out only in emergencies. But the marlinespike was a ship's tool, not a weapon. Similar to an ice pick in shape, it had a round wooden handle and a round blade with a sharp point and was used to separate strands of rope for making splices. It was both handy and deadly, and best of all for a mutineer, there were usually dozens of them on deck.

Ax. Used to cut grappling lines and repel boarders.

Gully. Simply, a big knife. The best-known gully was the boucan knife used by buccaneers to hunt wild pigs.

STANDARD PIRATE OUTFIT

Pirates weren't particular about their clothes, as long as they were comfortable and brightly colored. Here's what they wore:

- loose pants (often striped)
- cotton shirt
- sash (for pistols and daggers)
- loose jacket
- leather belt (to hold a cutlass)
- no shoes (Most sailors didn't wear shoes—leather soles were too slippery in bad weather.)
- gold earrings

ABOUT THOSE GOLD EARRINGS

Historians say that pirates believed that piercing their ears with gold and silver improved their eyesight at sea.

Can piercing your ears really improve your eyesight? According to some acupuncturists, the earlobe is an acupuncture point for several eye ailments, and there have been reports of people whose vision improved after having their ears pierced. But they don't recommend it, because scar tissue forms where the ear is pierced and blocks any further helpful effects.

*   *   *

A PIRATE MYTH: Walking the plank. Few (if any) pirate ships ever used the plank. Most pirates relied on the time-honored "heave-ho" method of getting rid of pesky prisoners—they just picked them up and tossed them overboard. *A-a-a-r-r-rgh!*

FART SONGS

*All right, kids, time to sing along with
Uncle John. Come on—it's a gas!*

TRAVELING FARTS

(to the tune of "Hello, Operator")
Going down the highway,
Doing eighty-four.
Johnny cut a gasser—
It blew me out the door!
The engine, it exploded.
The chassis fell apart.
All because of Johnny and his
Supersonic fart!

BLOWING IN THE WIND

(also to the tune of "Hello, Operator")
A little gush of wind,
Straight from the heart;
It trickled down my backbone,
And it's also called a fart.
A fart can be useful;
It gives the body ease,
It warms the bed in winter,
And suffocates the fleas.

Wash up! Proper hand-washing could save 1 million lives per year.

LOONEY LAWS

Believe it or not, these laws are real.

You can howl after 9:00 p.m. in Columbus, Georgia…but your cat can't.

Pharmacists in Trout Creek, Utah, cannot sell gunpowder as a headache medicine.

Hello? If you're under twelve and you live in Blue Earth, Minnesota, you must be accompanied by an adult when you talk on the phone.

In Eureka, Nevada, it is illegal for a man to kiss a woman if he has a mustache.

Canadians are forbidden from removing their bandages in public.

Hawaii residents can be fined for putting coins in their ears.

In Knoxville, Tennessee, it's against the law to lasso a fish.

Lawmakers in Boston, Massachusetts, have ruled that a pickle must bounce four inches when dropped from waist height.

Winston-Salem, North Carolina, will not allow children under the age of seven to go to college.

It is illegal to drive without a steering wheel in Decatur, Illinois.

You cannot pretend to practice witchcraft in Canada.

In Portland, Oregon, you cannot wear roller skates in a restroom or whistle under water.

Magic carpet: A high-quality Persian rug can last for 500 years.

CAPTAIN UNDERPANTS

You have to admire a guy who writes about talking toilets and names one of his books Captain Underpants and the Perilous Plot of Professor Poopy Pants.

THE EARLY YEARS

Dav Pilkey was born March 4, 1966, in Cleveland, Ohio, where he lived with his mom, dad, and sister. He loved to draw—so much so that while other kids were outside playing baseball and football, Dav (pronounced "Dave") was usually inside drawing monsters and superheroes. "Life was pretty cool when I was little," he says. "And then…school started."

THE HYPERACTIVE KID

• In elementary school, Dav spent a lot of time making funny noises, running around the classroom, and sticking crayons up his nose. His classmates loved it, but his teacher did not and regularly sent him out of the classroom.

• He actually set a record for most time spent in the principal's office. (He was later diagnosed with attention deficit disorder and severe hyperactivity, which explains why it was so hard for him to sit still.)

• Dav says he spent so much time in the hall during first grade that his teacher moved a little desk out there for him. It was at this desk that he first invented his ideal superhero—a guy who flew around

the city in his underwear giving wedgies to all the bad guys.

• Dav's second-grade teacher at St. John's Lutheran School happened to use the word *underpants* in class one day, and everyone started laughing. The teacher got mad and told the class that "underwear is not funny." Everyone laughed harder. That's when Dav realized that *underpants* was a very funny word, and that Captain Underpants would be a great name for a superhero.

• Dav's name was spelled "Dave" until he reached high school, when he got a weekend job working at Pizza Hut. The machine that made the nametags broke and couldn't print the letter "e," so his nametag read "Dav." He thought it was cool and has spelled it that way ever since.

DAV HITS THE BIG TIME

When Dav started college at Kent State University in Ohio, his English teacher told him she thought he was a good writer and she loved the pictures he drew. She suggested he try writing children's books, so he did.

His first book was *World War Won*, a story about two animal kings, each racing to build the tallest tower of nuclear weapons. When the kings realize that they are threatening not only themselves but their whole world, they seek help from the other animals.

Dav entered the book in a student writing contest—and won. *World War Won* was published in 1986, and Dav went on to become a very successful author. He has written other popular books, such as *Kat Kong* and *Dogzilla*, but it's his book series about George and Harold, two kids with attention deficit disorder and severe hyperactivity (like himself) that has been the biggest

The first picture books for children appeared in the 1600s.

success. The *Captain Underpants* books have won lots of awards and have sold more than 70 million copies worldwide!

The coolest thing about being a successful author, according to Dav: "I used to get in trouble for being the class clown…and now it's my job!"

*　　*　　*

TWO DUMB CROOKS

Crime #1: An Arkansas man decided to break into a liquor store by throwing a cinder block through the front window. He lifted the heavy block over his head and heaved it at the window.

Gotcha! Because the window was made of Plexiglas, the cinder block just bounced off…and knocked the thief unconscious. Adding insult to injury, the entire episode was recorded by a security camera.

Crime #2: Two nervous robbers burst into a Michigan record shop waving loaded revolvers. One of them yelled, "Nobody move!"

Gotcha! Someone moved—his partner. The other thief was so startled that he shot him.

Q: How can you tell a male turkey from a female? A: Only the males gobble.

ICE HOTELS

They're built in the middle of winter and last until spring.
When they're gone, there's nothing left but a puddle.
These crystal palaces are the snow forts of everyone's
dreams—and they're great places to chill out!

WHAT ARE THEY?

Ice hotels are exactly what they sound like—hotels made out of
ice. The floors and ceilings are ice. The beds, tables, and even
drinking glasses are made of ice. Your bed of ice is warm and cozy
because it's covered in reindeer skins and a down sleeping bag.
Your room might even have a Jacuzzi and a fireplace. There are
art galleries (featuring ice art) and movie theaters, ice chapels,
and snow restaurants. There's always one room that's not frozen,
however—the bathroom (you can't flush frozen water).

AN ICE IDEA

The first ice castle was built in Jukkasjarvi, Sweden, in 1990. It
wasn't really meant to be a hotel, but some people decided to
spend the night there and loved it. They spread the word, and now
there are four ice hotels around the world. No matter how cold it
gets outside, the temperature in an ice castle remains between 2°
and 24°F. That's because of the insulating properties of ice. Like
an igloo, ice castles retain the warmth from the people and other
heat sources inside. The retained heat melts the inside of the walls
and ceiling slightly, but the water quickly returns to ice. This thin
sheet of ice acts like a layer of cement, sealing out the cold and
holding in the heat.

Eskimos use refrigerators to keep food from freezing.

HOW ARE THEY BUILT?

Depending on the size of the structure, each hotel will use about 10,000 tons of ice and 10,000 to 30,000 tons of snow. An arched steel frame provides support for the walls, which are four feet thick. To create the vaulted ceilings, snow cannons and tractors mold snow over the frames. Finally, ice columns are put in place to provide extra support for the ceilings. The 60-room ice hotel in Sweden takes two months to build, but the builders start "harvesting" thousands of tons of ice for it in June.

With a room temperature hovering around 24°F, you probably won't be running around in your birthday suit. But with proper cold-weather clothing, the hotels are quite comfortable (so we've heard)…and beautiful!

Not all icebergs are white—some are green, some are black, and some are blue.

SECRET AGENT WOMAN

*Some spies are so secretive that their identities remain
unknown...even after they die. Agent 355 was
such a spy. Her life was filled with secrets,
lies, danger, love, and betrayal.*

I SPY

The year was 1776. The American colonies were fighting desperately
for their independence from England, and were trying every tactic
they could think of to win, including espionage. Secret spy rings,
like the Sons of Liberty and Knowlton's Rangers, formed to help
deliver vital information to the American military.

Major Benjamin Tallmadge, who was based in New York City
and Long Island, assembled his own top-flight group of spies
to supply the leader of the American troops, General George
Washington, with British military secrets.

SPY RING

Tallmadge hired a farmer named Abraham Woodhull to head the
spy ring. His code name was "Samuel Culper Sr." Woodhull's
best secret agent was Robert Townsend, whose code name was
"Samuel Culper Jr." They used only their code names in all their
correspondence with General Washington. The Culper Ring, as
it came to be known, became the most famous spy ring of the
American Revolution. They corresponded in invisible ink, wrote in

secret codes, and left information packets hidden in specific places to be picked up later by other agents.

MYSTERY WOMAN

The Culper Ring was constantly searching for more clever ways to gain access to British secrets. In 1778 Woodhull got the idea to recruit a woman for the job. Many of the colonists still socialized with the British officers, and one officer, Major André, was known for his love of pretty girls. What could be better than making one of these beautiful girls into a spy?

Woodhull found the perfect woman for the job. Who was she? No one knows. More than 200 years later, her identity remains a secret. Most historians think she was a member of a colonial family who were British sympathizers.

When the Culper Ring learned that the British had figured out their invisible ink formula, they switched to a numerical code. The code for New York was 727, Washington was 711, Woodhull was 722, and Townsend was 723. The mysterious woman was assigned 355—the only name by which she is known today.

355 + 723 = LOVE

Agents 355 and 723 (Townsend) fell in love during their years working together. She even became pregnant with Townsend's child. Sadly, their story does not have a happy ending: 355's luck ran out in 1780. Betrayed by Benedict Arnold, the most famous traitor in American history, she was captured by the British and held prisoner on the prison ship Jersey. After giving birth to a son, who was named Robert Townsend Jr., Agent 355 died in captivity.

THE WALL

Today, most U.S. secret agents work for the Central Intelligence Agency. At CIA headquarters in Langley, Virginia, there is a memorial wall for those agents who have died while in service as spies. Each life is represented by a star chiseled into the marble wall. As of 2004, there were 80 stars. Below the stars, protected in a glass case, a book of honor lists the names of only 46 of the 80 agents. The names of the other 34 will remain a secret forever—and Agent 355 is one of those secret stars.

* * *

IT'S BETTER THAN
RAYMOND RAYMOND RAYMOND

In 2004 a 39-year-old Illinois man named Raymond Allen Gray Jr. decided to change his name to Bubba. Bubba had been his nickname for years, so he figured he was just making it official. Soon after that, he decided to change his *middle* name to Bubba. And then he changed his *last* name, too. He's now legally known—and it's on his driver's license—as Bubba Bubba Bubba.

RICHIE'S TOYS

Kids can be anything they want to be. Look at Richie Stachowski.
He became a toy inventor when he was just 11 years old.

UNDERWATER CHALLENGE

In 1996 fifth-grader Richie Stachowski was snorkeling with his dad in Hawaii when he spotted some sea turtles. Richie was so amazed to see them that he shouted for his dad to look. But his dad couldn't hear Richie...because they were underwater.

That night Richie began thinking about inventing a way that people could talk to each other underwater. He sketched out some designs of an underwater megaphone in his hotel room and when he returned to California, researched underwater acoustics on the Internet. Then Richie built a model of his idea, using the $267 he had in his savings account. It looked something like a megaphone attached to a snorkel mouthpiece.

Richie tested his underwater megaphone in every bathtub and swimming pool he could find. Three months later, he had perfected his new invention: Water Talkies.

SHORT STACK

Richie's mother, Barbara, also an inventor and a businesswoman, helped Richie set up his own company. He called it Short Stack, after his favorite breakfast: pancakes. His company motto is "Made by a kid for kids." Soon Richie was selling his Water Talkies through Wal-Mart, KMart, Target, and Toys 'R' Us.

MORE INVENTIONS

The success of Water Talkies made Richie decide to create more toys. He invented the Bumper Jumper Water Pumper, a sit-down water float whose paddle doubles as a water gun, and the Aqua Scope, a periscope that lets snorkelers see under and above the water at the same time.

Three years and five more inventions later, Richie sold his company to Wild Planet Toys in San Francisco for—are you ready for this?—$7 *million*! And he was only 14 years old!

Try it: When an ice cube melts, it doesn't raise the water level in the glass.

"HELLO GIRLS"

The telephone has been around for more than a century,
but cell phones, dial tones, and automatic connections
are relatively new. So how did phone calls
get through before? The operator.

VOICE WITH A SMILE

When telephone service began in the late 1870s, every call had to go through an operator who physically connected one caller's line with another by plugging it in at a central switchboard. The first operators were teenage boys, most of whom were used to delivering telegrams as fast as they could on their bikes. (That was the speediest way to deliver messages before Alexander Graham Bell patented the telephone in 1876.) But these high-spirited boys were often rude to customers and to each other. More than once, phone service was "put on hold" as the boys cheered on a fistfight.

GIRL POWER

In an attempt to improve service, the early phone companies decided to do something drastic—employ women. Single girls between the ages of 17 and 20 were hired to replace the boys and became known as "hello girls," or "the voice with a smile."

On September 1, 1878, Emma M. Nutt became the very first hello girl when she went to work for the Boston Telephone

Despatch Company. As time went on, Emma and the other hello girls were expected to do more than just connect callers with another number. When someone called an operator, they might want to know the local time, a recipe, the weather report, or when the next train was scheduled to arrive. Some customers even asked for a wake-up call, or for the operator to listen for their baby crying while they went to visit a friend!

OPERATOR TO THE RESCUE!

The telephone became a lifeline for many people, especially out in the country, and the operator was there to help.

• Farmers would call with news of tornadoes, storms, or impending frosts, and the operators would phone the information to other farmers in time for them to round up livestock and protect crops.

• Many a story is told of heroic operators who remained at their posts to warn of floods and coordinate rescue efforts, even as the waters rose around their switchboards.

• A New Jersey operator once received a call from a panicked druggist, who said that a customer had walked off with a bottle of acid instead of eye drops. She started making calls—to relatives, the postmaster, and other subscribers. The operator finally reached the woman in a New York City hotel, just as she was unwittingly about to give her eyes an acid bath.

Today computers handle most of the work once done by operators, but some things never change—you can still reach a live operator if you need to, 24 hours a day.

OME ALONE GAMES

*Here are a few more great games to play on a
rainy day—or any day, for that matter.*

TABLETOP OBSTACLE COURSE

Object of the Game: To build your own obstacle course and
race against the clock.

Setup: You'll need a Ping-Pong ball, a straw, a felt-tip pen,
newspaper, tape, and some "obstacles," such as books, small toys,
some cups, and silverware. Cover a large table with the newspaper
and tape down the corners. Spread the obstacles out on the table.
Draw a course around and through them with the felt-tip pen.

How to Play: Place the Ping-Pong ball at the start of the course
and blow through the straw to get it rolling. Keep blowing and
don't touch the ball with the straw. Your goal is to roll the ball
through the course without touching it, without hitting any of the
obstacles, and without letting it fall off the table. For even more
excitement, time your run with a stopwatch to see who's the fastest.

COINS IN THE WATER

Object of the Game: To win the treasure by dropping a coin
directly on top of it.

Setup: You'll need bright nail polish, small coins, and a plastic
bucket. Paint a dab of nail polish on both sides of a coin. Fill
the bucket with water and drop the coin into the water. This is
the "treasure."

Q: What do they call checkers games in England? A: Draughts (pronounced "drafts").

How to Play: To win the game, all you have to do is drop another coin into the bucket so that it lands directly on top of the treasure. Sounds easy, doesn't it? Think again, treasure hunter! This is much more difficult than you might imagine.

If you don't win the treasure at first, don't give up. Leave the game set up, coins and all, and when you have some pocket change to spare, try again. In fact, leave it set up for as long as it takes to win—days, weeks, months. Once you land on the treasure, all of the money in the bucket is yours! Jackpot!

*   *   *

CALLING DR. BOOGER!

An Austrian doctor has given kids everywhere an official thumbs up—up their noses! In March 2004, lung specialist Dr. Friedrich Bischinger said that eating one's own boogers provides a boost to the body's immune system. "The nose is a filter in which a great deal of bacteria are collected, and when this mixture arrives in the intestines it works like a medicine." He went on to say that society's pressure against nose picking is actually harmful—and that children should be encouraged to pick and eat their boogers!

Q: What are Fabio, Elmo, Bingo, Chico, and...

JAMAICA BOBSLED

What has four blades, four men, no engine...
and goes 90 miles per hour?

THE HOTTEST TEAM ON ICE

Jamaica is a tiny tropical island in the Caribbean Sea. It has plenty of sun, surf, and sand. What it doesn't have? Snow. Despite its balmy weather and complete lack of snow, Jamaica sent a four-man bobsled team to compete in the 1988 Calgary Winter Olympics.

WHAT IS BOBSLEDDING?

The bobsled was invented in Switzerland in 1897. The Swiss took *toboggans*, which are long, flat-bottomed sleds, and put runners on them to make them travel at high speeds down the famous Cresta Run at St. Moritz. Within a year, bobsled racing had become the new extreme winter sport in Europe. It got its name because early racers thought they could gain even more speed by "bobbing" their bodies back and forth in unison. Even though riders discovered later that that wasn't really true, the name stuck.

Nowadays, the sleds, or "bobs," are made of fiberglass and skate on four runners, which can be steered. The course is an ice track that looks like a giant waterslide. It's 1,640 yards long with between 15 and 20 banked turns.

To get moving, the team pushes the bobsled with a running start. Then they quickly hop into it and tuck in their heads for the

ride downhill. The push start is the most important part of the race. A great start can help a sled reach speeds of 90 mph.

Bobsledding became an official Olympic event in 1924, and over the years many countries have sent sled teams to compete in the Winter Games. But the most unusual—and attention-getting— by far was the first team from Jamaica.

THE BIG PUSH!

The guys on the Jamaican team were fast sprinters, which is important for a fast start in bobsledding. A few of them were even racing champions—pushcart racing champions.

Pushcarts are used throughout Jamaica as roving restaurants or shops. The four-wheeled carts are pushed onto street corners or to the side of the road and then opened for business. In 1975 a group of Jamaicans thought it would be fun to race their carts. With a driver steering and a runner pushing, the Push Cart Derby was born.

It was only a matter of time before someone recognized the similarity between the Jamaican Pushcart Derby and bobsled racing, and decided to form a team with push cart racers.

ISLAND TRAINING

There were a few big problems: no snow, no ice, and no bobsled. But hey! The team was cool, mon! They pushed their own wheeled version of a sled over dirt and sand, all around the island. They even took turns standing in a walk-in freezer to get used to cold weather—although nothing could really prepare them for Calgary, Canada, in the dead of winter.

Zoo-laska: 12,000 years ago, elephants, lions, and camels lived in Alaska.

COOL RUNNINGS

Using a real bobsled, on real ice for the first time in their lives, the Jamaican team entered the 1988 Olympic bobsled competition. They careened, they crashed, and they finished dead last.

But the Jamaicans inspired other tropical countries, such as Trinidad and Tobago, Puerto Rico, and the Virgin Islands to join the bobsled competition. They're the team that inspired the 1993 movie, *Cool Runnings*. And they won the hearts of everyone watching them race. Why? As team member Devon Harris explained, "When you think of Jamaica, you think of sun and surf. When you think of Jamaican bobsled, a smile comes across your face."

* * *

I SPY A JOKE

Q: What do you call an underwater secret agent?
A: James Pond

Q: What do you call a secret agent with dyed hair?
A: James Blond

Two spies walk into a bar. One spy begins a joke, then says to the other, "I'm sorry, your security clearance isn't high enough to hear the punchline."

Q: How do spies sleep?
A: Undercover

Q: How are spies and pilots alike?
A: They're both masters of disguise (the skies).

AMAZING KIDS

These amazing kids prove that all you need to change the world is a good idea and some follow through. Go for it!

BOOK IT

Amazing Kid: Brandon Keefe, age 8, West Hills, California

Big Idea: BookEnds, a nonprofit organization that donates children's books to schools and youth organizations in the Los Angeles area.

How He Did It: In 1993 Brandon heard through his mother that Hollygrove, a home for abused kids, was building a library but had no money to buy books. Brandon came up with a solution. He figured that every kid at his elementary school had at least one book that they didn't want, so he organized a book drive. Four months later, Brandon surprised his mom by donating 847 new and slightly used books to the children's library at Hollygrove. Since then, BookEnds has donated more than half a million books to 120 children's libraries.

IT'S IN THE BAG

Amazing Kid: Josh Marcus, age 10, Boca Raton, Florida

Big Idea: Sack It to You, a project that provides backpacks filled with school supplies to needy kids.

How He Did It: It all began in 1996 when Josh paid a visit to a daycare center for the children of migrant workers. When he asked how he could help, he was told the kids needed backpacks for school. He started collecting them from friends and neighbors. Then he contacted businesses like Office Depot for more help.

Since then, Josh has helped thousands of children through his organization. Sack It to You has raised over $400,000 and given away more than 9,000 backpacks to disadvantaged kids in south Florida and around the country. Josh still hand delivers most of the Florida backpacks himself!

TOP HAT

Amazing Kid: Anthony Leanna, age 10, Suamico, Wisconsin

Big Idea: Heavenly Hats, a community service program that collects and distributes brand-new hats to cancer patients who have lost their hair.

How He Did It: In May 2001, Anthony got the idea when his grandmother lost her hair while undergoing chemotherapy treatment for breast cancer. He made posters and placed hat collection boxes in downtown businesses. He also e-mailed and telephoned businesses around the world, asking for donations. As of January 2004, Anthony had sent more than 20,000 hats to more than 90 hospitals and clinics across the United States.

...It took him 4 years, 3 months, 16 days, and 21 pairs of shoes.

THE MAGIC HORSE

We told you about the Chimera in our first Bathroom Reader for Kids Only. Here's the Greek myth of how it met its end.

Bellerophon was a very brave young man who had only one fault—he was handsome. So handsome that Queen Anteia, the wife of King Proteus, fell in love with him. King Proteus was wild with jealousy and rage, but he hid it from one and all.

Calmly, the king asked Bellerophon to do him a great favor and deliver a letter to Queen Anteia's father, King Iobates of Lycia.

Bellerophon was happy to help the king. He delivered the letter without knowing that the message inside was a note from Proteus asking Iobates to murder Bellerophon.

But Iobates didn't want the blood of this young man on his hands. Instead, he sent Bellerophon on a seemingly impossible mission, one that would surely end in the young man's death. He ordered Bellerophon to kill the Chimera—a ferocious beast that had been terrorizing his kingdom.

The Chimera was three monsters in one! It had the fire-breathing head of a lion and the body of a goat. Its tail was a snake with venom so poisonous that it could kill with one bite.

Bellerophon was frightened and went to ask the wise man Polyidus for help. "Please wise sir, I am just a man. How can I fight such a dreadful creature?"

"You cannot do it alone," Polyidus advised. "You will need the help of Pegasus, the flying horse. He is the only creature who can survive the Chimera's fiery breath."

But how could Bellerophon even approach this magnificent beast?

"Go to the temple," the wiseman told him. "Pray to Athena. She will help you."

Bellerophon did as he was told, and that night while he slept, Athena came to him Pegasus. He found the wild horse grazing by the well, just as Athena had told him. The golden bridle was magical, so the instant Pegasus saw it, he became tame. He trotted over and touched Bellerophon's shoulder with his nose.

in his dream. She placed a golden bridle in his hand and told him how to find the well where Pegasus drank.

When Bellerophon awoke, he hurried to find Bellerophon placed the bridle on Pegasus and mounted his back. He clicked his tongue and they were airborne. "To the Chimera, Pegasus!" he shouted. "And may the goddess Athena watch over us!"

The beautiful white horse flew them to the Chimera's cave. Armed with a long spear, Bellerophon charged the Chimera.

The monster exhaled its horrible fire, but Pegasus danced away from the burning breath. Before the Chimera could breathe again, Pegasus flew close and Bellerophon drove his spear through the Chimera's heart.

The triumphant duo, Bellerophon and Pegasus, flew back to King Iobates' palace. When the people saw the young hero carrying the head of the Chimera, they were ecstatic. King Iobates, too, was pleased...and amazed. Bellerophon had achieved the impossible task and saved the kingdom.

Not only did Iobates spare Bellerophon's life, he gave the handsome young man a handsome reward— the hand of his youngest daughter in marriage.

They lived together happily and when Iobates died, Bellerophon became king. That should have been enough to satisfy any man, but Bellerophon longed for greater adventures and decided to fly Pegasus to Mount Olympus and visit the gods.

But Bellerophon's arrogance displeased Zeus, king of the gods, for no one but the gods were permitted on Mount Olympus.

"Impudent mortal," he thundered, and sent a tiny fly to punish him. The fly stung Pegasus. The horse reared, hurling Bellerophon off his back.

Athena spared Bellerophon. He landed on soft ground. But for the rest of his life, he walked the land, lonely and crippled, in search of his magnificent steed.

Alas...the winged Pegasus never returned.

VIDEO TREASURES

Next time you're at a video store with no idea what to rent, here are a few recommendations.

THE MAN WHO WOULD BE KING (1975) *Adventure*

"Old-fashioned adventure and derring-do. Two British soldier-pals try to bamboozle high priests of remote Kafiristan into turning over their riches by convincing them that one of them is a god. The acting is ideal, the script is superb, and the film is entertaining." (*Leonard Maltin's Movie & Video Guide*)

SPLASH (1984) *Comedy*

"An uproarious comedy about a young man (Tom Hanks) who unwittingly falls in love with a mermaid (Daryl Hannah). Marvelous." (*Video Movie Guide*)

THE LAST STARFIGHTER (1984) *Science Fiction*

"A teenage video game whiz is abducted by the survivors of a distant planet who need his skills to outwit their enemies. Sharp and witty." (*Halliwell's Video Guide*)

BILLY ELLIOT (2000) *Comedy/Drama*

"Living in working-class England, Billy is allowed to take boxing as a sport but his eyes are on the dance class next door. The dance instructor notices his interest and invites him to dance. He does—quite badly—but over time he improves. This film does well in showing a young man's enthusiasm for dance and how he's able to win acceptance through perseverance." (*Scarecrow Video Movie Guide*)

WE DIG TUT!

Uncle John has often wondered what exactly was in King Tut's tomb—besides his mummy. Here's the answer.

TUT'S TOMB

In 1922, after five long years of digging in the Valley of the Kings, Egypt's famous graveyard of the pharaohs, British archaeologist Howard Carter and wealthy financier Lord Carnarvon finally found what they were searching for—the lost tomb of King Tutankhamen, or King Tut for short. The young pharaoh had become ruler of all Egypt when he was only 9 years old, and died when he was 18. He had been buried for more than 3,000 years when his tomb was discovered.

BEHIND DOOR NUMBER ONE

The tomb consisted of four rooms, each filled with amazing artifacts. The British explorers entered the antechamber, or outer room, first. There they found two life-size statues of King Tut dressed in gold, a golden throne, and many elaborately carved golden beds. A stack of chariot parts filled one corner, and the chamber was piled floor to ceiling with gilded dishes, painted statues, and furniture.

The entrance to another room, known as the annex, was found under a golden bed with carved hippopotamus heads. The annex was crammed with more than 2,000 everyday objects, including baskets of food, fans, finger rings, daggers, shields, shoes, eye makeup, and wine jars. There was even a box filled with 150 pairs of underwear!

On a roll: The first wheeled vehicles were invented around 3500 B.C.

GOLDEN BOY

At the center of the third room, the *burial chamber*, was a huge wooden box covered in gold. Inside was a carved stone coffin called a *sarcophagus*. And inside that were three nested coffins, each one more elaborately decorated than the other. The last coffin, which held King Tut's mummified body, was made of solid gold and weighed 296 pounds!

The mummy was wearing sandals made of gold, 140 golden bracelets and rings, and a collar made from 171 gold pieces. His face and shoulders were covered in a beautifully crafted gold mask that weighs 22 pounds. The mask is priceless, but the gold used to make it would be worth $140,000 in today's money. The gold from the coffin is valued at about $2 million. It was worth a lot in Tut's day, too—all that gold would have bought 1,600 cows, 5,000 donkeys, or 50,000 goats!

Bottoms up! The Nile catfish swims upside down.

TREASURES GALORE

The fourth chamber of King Tut's tomb was called the treasury because it contained even more riches than the other three rooms.

Towering above the treasures was a gold-covered shrine protected by statues of goddesses. Inside the shrine were King Tut's vital organs—his heart, liver, and lungs—each individually wrapped in linen and placed in its own little coffin.

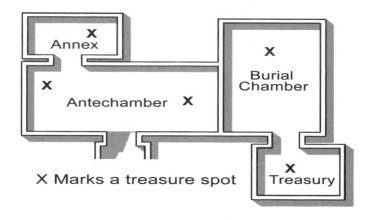

X Annex

X Burial Chamber

X Antechamber X

X Marks a treasure spot

X Treasury

TUT'S LEGACY

Surprisingly, in his time, young King Tut wasn't considered an important pharaoh and was forgotten soon after his death. That may be why his tomb wasn't looted of its treasures as so many others were. Instead it lay unnoticed until Howard Carter found it. But now more than 2.5 million people visit King Tut's treasures at the Egyptian Museum in Cairo each year, making him the best-known pharaoh in history.

Some mummies have tattoos.

WHAT'S YOUR SIGN?

Uncle John's astrological sign is Taurus (maybe that's why people say he's bullheaded). What's yours?

♈ ARIES (MARCH 21-APRIL 20)
The Ram

Element: Fire   **Metal:** Iron

Statement: "I am."   **Flower:** Honeysuckle

Gemstone: Diamond   **Color:** Red

Characteristics: Aries are natural leaders, energetic, and fun-loving. If you're an Aries, your friends can count on you to rally everyone for an adventure. But you get bored easily and your temper comes and goes—in a flash! Above all, you are a pioneer; just give others a chance to catch up with you every now and then.

Born Under Aries: *Johann Sebastian Bach, Reese Witherspoon, Norah Jones, Sheryl Swoopes, Peyton Manning, Vincent van Gogh, Jackie Chan, Maya Angelou, Kate Hudson, Colin Powell, Thomas Jefferson, Aretha Franklin, Eddie Murphy, Leonardo da Vinci*

♉ TAURUS (APRIL 21-MAY 21)
The Bull

Element: Earth   **Metal:** Copper

Statement: "I have."   **Flower:** Daisy

Gemstone: Emerald   **Color:** Pastels

Characteristics: Though friends may think you're stubborn, you're just committed to doing things your own way. The Taurus mind works like a clock: methodically, carefully, and decisively. You're patient, warmhearted, and loving. Practical and reliable, you can be counted on to get the job done—at your own pace, of course.

Born Under Taurus: *Queen Elizabeth II, Andre Agassi, William Shakespeare, Kelly Clarkson, Barbra Streisand, Florence Nightingale, Jerry Seinfeld, Kirsten Dunst, George Clooney, Malcolm X, Tim McGraw, Ella Fitzgerald, Tony Hawk, Harry Truman, George Lucas, Janet Jackson, Cher*

♊ GEMINI (MAY 22-JUNE 21)
The Twins

Element: Air   **Metal:** Mercury

Statement: "I think."   **Flower:** Lavender

Gemstone: Agate   **Color:** Yellow

Characteristics: Geminis are full of ideas and love to talk about them. You can settle arguments between friends and make them laugh at the same time. Your parents will never worry if you're reading enough—you're probably reading three or four books right now! Your mood can change on a whim, which may make you seem a little wishy-washy. But in reality, you just love to do everything at once.

Born Under Gemini: *Wild Bill Hickock, Michael J. Fox, John F. Kennedy, Clint Eastwood, Paula Abdul, the Olsen twins, Allen Iverson, Marilyn Monroe, Alanis Morissette, Venus Williams,*

Johnny Depp, Judy Garland, Mike Myers, Courtney Cox, Nicole Kidman, Prince William

 ## CANCER (JUNE 22-JULY 22)
The Crab

Element: Water

Statement: "I feel."

Gemstone: Pearl

Metal: Silver

Flower: White rose

Color: Silvery blue

Characteristics: Cancers are the zodiac's caregivers and make great doctors and nurses. If your sign is Cancer, you love comfort, tradition, and family. You're also artistic, creative, and sensitive. Cancers often are the first to laugh and the first to cry. Even so, you're no pushover. You like to get your own way and will fight for a good cause.

Born Under Cancer: *Tobey Maguire, Helen Keller, Liv Tyler, Missy Elliot, Princess Diana, George W. Bush, Nelson Mandela, Tom Cruise, Nancy Reagan, P. T. Barnum, Michelle Kwan, Tom Hanks, Bill Cosby, George Washington Carver, Robin Williams, Kristi Yamaguchi*

 ## LEO (JULY 23-AUGUST 23)
The Lion

Element: Fire

Statement: "I will."

Gemstone: Peridot

Metal: Gold

Flower: Sunflower

Color: Yellow

Characteristics: Leos are strong, proud, and powerful. You're also funny and dramatic, which is why a life in the theater

Vandalism or history? Archaeologists often find ancient graffiti on excavated walls.

is a natural choice for you. Leos are the life of every party. A bit self-centered, you hate to be ignored. When this happens, you may become the wounded lion. Just remember, it's your charm, not your temper, that brings you the attention you love.

Born Under Leo: *Jacqueline Kennedy Onassis, Amelia Earhart, Alex Rodriguez, Beatrix Potter, Henry Ford, Lucille Ball, Gary Larson, Neil Armstrong, Napoléon, J. K. Rowling, Annie Oakley, Magic Johnson, Madonna, Meriwether Lewis, Arnold Schwarzenegger, Bill Clinton*

♍ VIRGO (AUGUST 24-SEPTEMBER 23)
The Virgin

Element: Earth **Metal:** Mercury

Statement: "I analyze." **Flower:** Buttercup

Gemstone: Sapphire **Color:** Navy

Characteristics: Virgos are shy, sweet, and sympathetic. You are also honest, reliable, and down-to-earth. If you are a Virgo, you love to take things apart and put them back together. You also love your time alone—the perfect time to read and think. Even though you might get bogged down by details, you are devoted to working toward the greater good of all.

Born Under Virgo: Gloria Estefan, John McCain, Pink, Michael Jackson, Mother Teresa, Dr. Phil, LeAnn Rimes, Ani DiFranco, Bruce Springsteen, Cameron Diaz, Beyoncé Knowles, Keanu Reeves, Jesse James, Andy Roddick, Faith Hill, Lance Armstrong, Stephen King, Adam Sandler

Rats can't barf.

LIBRA (SEPTEMBER 24-OCTOBER 23)
The Scales

Element: Air

Metal: Copper

Statement: "I balance."

Flower: Rose

Gemstone: Opal

Color: Blue

Characteristics: Extremely social, Libras love to talk, have many friends, and are very smart. Libras dislike conflict and want everyone to be happy. When it comes to your own life, you weigh everything carefully, which sometimes makes it difficult for you to make up your mind. You're happiest when you're with family and friends, and everyone is getting along.

Born Under Libra: *Kate Winslet, Jim Henson, Eminem, Bernie Mac, Christopher Reeve, Eleanor Roosevelt, Jimmy Carter, Michelle Wie, Vlggo Mortensen, Noah Webster, Julie Andrews, Mahatma Gandhi, Will Smith, Brett Favre, Matt Damon, Gwen Stefani, Donna Karan, Alfred Nobel*

 SCORPIO (OCTOBER 24-NOVEMBER 22)
The Scorpion

Element: Water

Metal: Steel

Statement: "I desire."

Flower: Geranium

Gemstone: Topaz

Color: Maroon

Characteristics: People see Scorpios as mysterious, and you like it that way. When they look into your piercing eyes, you fix them with your hypnotic gaze. You love to listen and learn everything you can about others. In fact, you'd make a good spy. No one can tell you what to do, and while this stubborn determination might get you into trouble, it will also help you succeed. Your friends love your quiet wisdom, honesty, and fierce loyalty.

Born Under Scorpio: *Julia Roberts, Bill Gates, Hillary Rodham Clinton, Jonas Salk, Winona Ryder, Marie Curie, P. Diddy, Daniel Boone, Sammy Sosa, Peter Jackson, Carl Sagan, Marie Antoinette, Bjork, Leonardo DiCaprio, Jack Osbourne, Robert Louis Stevenson, Condoleezza Rice*

 ## SAGITTARIUS (NOV 23-DEC 21)
The Archer

Element: Fire

Statement: "I see."

Gemstone: Turquoise

Metal: Tin

Flower: Dandelion

Color: Purple

Characteristics: Sagittarians have so much creative energy that it's hard for them to sit still. You throw yourselves into one adventure after another and would make a good pilot or race car driver. Smart and funny, you love to learn but sometimes get bored. There might be a trail of unfinished chores behind you. You'll find satisfaction when you learn to complete a project before hurling yourself into the next one.

Born Under Sagittarius: *Billy the Kid, Charles Schulz, Nelly Furtado, Donovan McNabb, Mark Twain, Bruce Lee, Louisa May Alcott, C. S. Lewis, Ben Stiller, Jay–Z, Tyra Banks, Brad Pitt, Lucy Liu, Walt Disney, Beethoven, Christina Aguilera, Frankie Muniz, Steven Spielberg*

Small talk: There are a quadrillion *femtoseconds* in one second.

CAPRICORN (DEC 22-JAN 20)

The Goat

Element: Earth

Statement: "I use."

Gemstone: Garnet

Metal: Silver

Flower: Pansy

Color: Brown

Characteristics: Think of a nimble goat that scrambles to the top of the mountain—that's a Capricorn. Capricorns like to succeed and make solid leaders. In fact, many people think you're older than you really are. On the outside you're the strong, silent type; inside, you're a mushy romantic. You love school. You respect authority and honor tradition. You are ambitious and will work hard to get ahead.

Born Under Capricorn: *Sir Isaac Newton, Betsy Ross, Denzel Washington, LeBron James, Mel Gibson, J.R.R. Tolkien, Joan of Arc, Nicolas Cage, Elvis Presley, Mary J. Blige, Dave Matthews, Martin Luther King, Jim Carrey, Muhammed Ali, Benjamin Franklin, A.A. Milne*

AQUARIUS (JANUARY 21-FEBRUARY 19)
The Water Bearer

Element: Air

Statement: "I know."

Gemstone: Aquamarine

Metal: Aluminum

Flower: Orchid

Color: Turquoise

Characteristics: Aquarians are visionaries and love thinking about how to make things better. You know how to share your ideas and how to inspire your friends. Even though you're friendly

Mouse meat was considered a delicacy in ancient China and parts of India.

and interested in people, you value your privacy. You also have a silly, unpredictable side, which has led some to describe you as half Albert Einstein, half Mickey Mouse!

Born Under Aquarius: *Wayne Gretzky, Ronald Reagan, Oprah Winfrey, Ellen DeGeneres, Thomas Edison, Elijah Wood, Alicia Keys, Justin Timberlake, Hank Aaron, Babe Ruth, Sheryl Crow, Charles Lindbergh, Abraham Lincoln, Jennifer Aniston, Charles Darwin, Rosa Parks, Matt Groening, Ashton Kutcher*

 ## PISCES (FEBRUARY 20-MARCH 20)
The Fish

Element: Water   **Metal:** Platinum

Statement: "I believe."   **Flower:** Water lily

Gemstone: Amethyst   **Color:** Sea green

Characteristics: Pisces are dreamers. Charming and compassionate, you're also intuitive; you often know what's needed before anyone else is aware that there's a problem. But you see the world through rose-colored glasses and believe in the good of all beings. You might paint a picture, write a book, or sing and dance in celebration. You have the soul of a true artist.

Born Under Pisces: *Charlotte Church, Drew Barrymore, Steve Irwin, George Washington, Steve Jobs, Sean Astin, Buffalo Bill Cody, Shaquille O'Neal, Chelsea Clinton, Dr. Seuss, Ruth Bader Ginsburg, Queen Latifah, Andrew Jackson, Wyatt Earp, Mr. Rogers, Mia Hamm, Michelangelo, Dakota Fanning, Albert Einstein*

INTO THE FUTURE

Well, here we are at the end of another Bathroom Reader FOR KIDS ONLY. Wasn't it great? (Thank you!) Here are some words to send you off...into the future.

"The best way to predict the future is to create it."
—**Alan Kay, computer scientist**

"My interest is in the future because I am going to spend the rest of my life there."
—**Charles F. Kettering, inventor**

"It's never too late to have a happy childhood."
—**Jerry Seinfeld**

"I never think of the future. It comes soon enough."
—**Albert Einstein**

"The future will be better tomorrow."
—**Dan Quayle, former vice president**

"The future belongs to those who believe in the beauty of their dreams."
—**Eleanor Roosevelt**

"Real generosity toward the future consists in giving all to what is present."
—**Albert Camus, writer**

"Enjoy present pleasures in such a way as not to injure future ones."
—**Seneca, Native American chief**

"There's a moment coming. It's not here yet. It's still on the way. It's in...*the future!* It hasn't arrived! Here it comes! Here it is...It's gone."
—**George Carlin**

ANSWERS

SECRET MESSAGE
(Answer from page 64)

KIDS RULE, ADULTS DROOL!

WORDPLAY PUZZLES
(Answers from page 119)

1. Head over heels

2. Made in China

3. Three Blind Mice
(no i's)

4. Excuse me

5. You're under arrest

6. Repeat after me

7. Missing link

8. Free-for-alls (four all's)

9. Wise guy

10. Big fish in a little pond

11. Niagara Falls

12. Polka dot underwear

13. History repeats itself

CHANGELINGS
(Answers from page 198)

Poor	Pig	Tears
Boor	Wig	Sears
Book	Wag	Stars
Rook	Way	Stare
Rock	Say	Stale
Rick	Sty	Stile
Rich		Smile

RESOURCE GUIDE

Hey! We're not done yet! Now's your chance to take it beyond the pages by checking out some of these:

WHERE YOU CAN LEARN TO TREE CLIMB

Tree Climbers International
P.O. Box 5588
Atlanta, GA 31107 USA
Email: tci@treeclimbing.com

TCI has 5 branches (pardon the pun!) called *groves* in the US, as well as in France, England, Germany, Japan, and Botswana.

FOR SANDBOARDERS

Deacon and Hilary Matthews of Florence, Oregon, took 40 acres of clean, fine-grained sand and sculpted it into long dunes, cliffs, giant bowls, chutes, and towers.

Sand Master Park
87542 Hwy 101
North Florence, OR 97439
Phone: (541) 997-6006

WANT TO FIND AN ICE HOTEL?

- L'Hôtel de Glace, Montmorency Falls, Quebec, Canada
- Snow Castle, Kemi, Lapland
- Ice Hotel, Jukkasjarvi, Sweden
- Crystalline Igloo Hotel, Greenland

THE LAST PAGE

FELLOW BATHROOM READERS:

Bathroom reading should never be taken loosely—we must sit firmly for what we believe in, even while the rest of the world is taking pot shots at us.

Sit Down and Be Counted! Join the Bathroom Readers' Institute. It's free! Send a self-addressed, stamped envelope to: BRI, P.O. Box 1117, Ashland, Oregon 97520. Or contact us through our website at *www.bathroomreader.com.* You'll receive a free membership card, our BRI newsletter (sent out via e-mail), discounts when ordering directly through the BRI, and you'll earn a permanent spot on the BRI honor roll!

UNCLE JOHN'S NEXT *BATHROOM READER FOR KIDS ONLY* IS IN THE WORKS!

Don't fret—there's more good reading on the way.

Is there a subject you'd like to see us research? Write to us or contact us through our website and let us know. We aim to please.

Well, we're out of space, and when you've got to go, you've got to go. Hope to hear from you soon. Meanwhile, remember:

Go with the Flow!